The Labelling Phenomenon:
Volume Two

Jack R Ernest

Copyright

Introduction

This is the fourth edition of the second volume of the initial book "The Labelling Phenomenon."

I must assert that I deliberately try to repeat things in different ways in order to make things easier to understand.

"An old friend once told me something that gave me great comfort. Something he had read. He said that Mozart, Beethoven, and Chopin never died. They simply became music."- Westworld.

"In a world where death is the hunter, my friend, there is no time for regrets or doubts. There is only time for decisions." - Carlos Castaneda.

Labelling

"When you label me, you negate me." - Soren Kierkegaard.

Man is damned to be labelled. Traditional sociologists only apply labelling theory to the criminals. The reality is that it should be applied to everyone.

The price one must pay for living (choosing) is that we become labelled.

How you are labelled is a component of your psyche.

That we can see and use language gives birth to a two-dimensional field of perception I call the Labelling Phenomenon. Think of the Labelling Phenomenon as a two-dimensional field, consisting of eyesight and language combining to produce something new. This is what we as human beings perceive the world to be. We think we just see the world through our sight. The reality is that language is added to this sight to produce something new I term the Labelling Phenomenon. Space time is the four-dimensional fabric of the universe. The Labelling Phenomenon is a two-dimensional fabric of eyesight and language. Both things combine to give the world we, as humans, perceive it as.

The Labelling Phenomenon: We are always analysing our environment. We are always labelling what we see. We are labelling people; they in turn are labelling us. We are dividing things into positive or negative; acceptable or unacceptable; appropriate or inappropriate. This is done with people but also with other things such as cars driving on the road. You have Conscious Labelling and Unconscious Labelling. Conscious Labelling is labelling someone a friend or a deviant.

Unconscious Labelling is when you are labelling those you do not know but interact with, such as walking up a street in a city. Despite the fact you do not know these people, you are labelling their behaviour. But it is unconscious, so you do not realize you are labelling them.

Language and eyesight combine to give the world as we know it. Remove one of them or perhaps both and the system changes. They combine to give birth to a two-dimensional Labelling Phenomenon in which we live in.

Conformity, narcissism, schizophrenia and so on are just responses to this phenomenon, they are a response to labelling. If our eyes detected light in a different manner, the Labelling Phenomenon would be different and hence the economic system would be different. This is also true of language. If we used a different type of language to communicate, we would perceive the world differently and consequently the economic system would change.

Animals, those other than humans, can only deal with sight. With humans, language is added to sight, to create the Labelling Phenomenon. This creates a highly volatile concoction.

"In a world full of danger, to be a potentially seeable object is to be constantly exposed to danger. Self-consciousness, then, may be the apprehensive awareness of oneself as potentially exposed to danger by the simple fact of being visible to others. The obvious defence against such a danger is to make oneself invisible in one way or another." - R.D. Laing

You need both eyesight and language to create the human Labelling Phenomenon. If we had no eyesight, this phenomenon, this two-dimensional field would not exist. If we only had eyesight and no language, we would be like all other animals.

Conformity, schizophrenia and narcissism are responses to society, to the Labelling Phenomenon. If we could not use language and if we saw in a different wavelength/frequency of light (if we saw the world in infrared), schizophrenia would probably not develop.

The Labelling Anxiety: As a result of the Labelling Phenomenon, we fear being negatively labelled. This fear I call the Labelling Anxiety. It could be people we know or people we don't know. This fear of being negatively labelled controls our behaviour. We strive to retrieve or maintain a positive label. We strive to avoid a negative label.

The Labelling Bind: Because of the Labelling Anxiety we get coerced, influenced or manipulated into doing certain things. We may not want to do something, but the threat of a negative label makes us do that certain something. For example, a friend invites you out. But you don't wish to go. However, because you realize that if you do not go, your friend will think you are rude and hence will negatively label you, you are compelled to go, to avoid this negative label.

The Labelling Chain Reaction: Being known (labelled by one person) can make us be labelled by more people. Being known by people, leads to being known by more people, which in turn leads to fearing being negatively labelled by these new people. For example, we fear a negative label from a friend who invites us out (Labelling Anxiety). This motivates us to meet up with this friend, even though we do not want to (Labelling Bind). Then when we meet up with this friend, we may get introduced to even more people and so begins a cycle or pattern, whereby we repeat the Labelling Anxiety and Labelling Bind with these new people.

The Labelling Conflict: Often there is a clash between desire (and other things) and being labelled. One wants sex but can be negatively labelled because of it. The woman who is promiscuous gets negatively labelled. The same applies to the hunt for money, in that it can lead to a bad reputation. The man who sells drugs to earn a living, gets labelled a criminal. Or maybe someone has unique views, which when expressed, lead to a negative label by society. Or maybe a latent homosexual is afraid to disclose his sexuality because he fears a negative label from family and friends.

When you become known, you become labelled and thus try to be emotionally vindicated by the person who knows you. You become caged by their opinion of you. You lose your freedom and commit existential suicide.

When you know someone (perhaps a co-worker) and they know you, you are put under pressure by them. Now apply this logic to family and friends. They put us under duress to behave a certain way.

The female in order to receive positive verification from the male must be attractive. The male in order to receive positive verification from the female must be attractive. What they do not realize is that their behaviour is unconsciously influenced by the herd. They live to placate the herd; to be positively labelled by the herd because they feel good when they are. Thus, to be known is to be condemned. Thus, there is no such thing as a positive label. Thus, people are not free.

Our unconscious mind is working round the clock. All behaviour is being divided into positive/acceptable/appropriate or negative/unacceptable/inappropriate. We do this even with people we do not know.

Men and women both command each other. Men in order to receive positive affirmation from a girlfriend or wife must concede. They must repress their instinctive drive. Women too must adapt to propitiate the boyfriend or husband. Through labelling, society regulates the individual and the individual regulates society. Why are men and women obsessed with vanity or beauty? They are because that is how they react to the Labelling Phenomenon. That is how they respond to being known and being labelled. This is how they neutralize the Labelling Anxiety brought on by the Labelling Phenomenon. A lot of our happiness and despair is linked to labelling. A man may want the woman of his dreams to like him, which is another way of saying he wants her to positively endorse him. Imagine for instance then that this said man rapes the woman. Now she negatively labels him. Our lives are lost in a battle of labels and it is a battle we cannot win.

Capitalistic society is a product of conflict, of friction, of competition, of envy etc. The Labelling Field is a battlefield. Where you live, where you do your shopping, where you work and so on, a perpetual sociological struggle is taking place to be appropriately labelled. The product of that endless feud is a functioning society. For example, you will be rejected by someone if you don't attend their wedding, if you ignore them, if you commit a crime etc. You will be ostracized by that person or persons. Thus, one must always validate and be validated; they must always approve and be approved. The battle manifests itself as the striving to be labelled positively by those you interact with, regardless of whether you know them or not. The war is a labelling war and it is all around us.

Truly, what we yearn to do, is expose ourselves to the herd and be accepted at the same time. That is essentially what habitual life boils down to. In everything we do and say, we want to be labelled positively. For example, the homosexual wishes to expose his identity to society and also wishes to be accepted for who he is at the same time. He wants to expose his identity to the herd and not be shunned.

It is humiliation, specifically the threat of humiliation, that drives society. From language comes opinion and from opinion comes humiliation. So language is a component in society's functionality.

I do not think we realize that everyone we meet is another individual who sociologically incarcerates us.

The Labelling Phenomenon is like space time. Gravity according to Einstein is not a force but is simply matter warping the fabric of spacetime. Likewise, society controls society through labelling. When you are walking up a busy street, you are controlling the behaviour of the people you see through labelling; they in turn are controlling you through labelling also. But it is unconscious. The very fact that you see them and they you, controls both you and them. But you cannot see this mechanism, only its response.

The economic system is a product of the Labelling Phenomenon.

We are moulded by opinion which means we are moulded by language.

We understand physical violence. But what of psychological violence? What if knowing people was violence upon your conscience? We conform because of psychological violence in the form of being labelled. Because of the Labelling Phenomenon, interpretation becomes a form of psychological assault. Being known is in fact violence upon our conscience, much like if we came face to face with a lion that has not eaten in a week. We are continuously being bombarded with one's interpretation of us.

In much the same vein that traffic accidents are caused by the close proximity of cars to each other, psychological violence is caused by people knowing each other. Every person that knows you, interprets you and this interpretation is a form of malice upon your conscience.

If you affiliate yourself with the herd, you deprive yourself of your freedom. We are all gods and devils. It is just a matter of interpretation. The world you see around you, live in and perhaps die in, is moulded by the Labelling Phenomenon.

You have to go back millions of years to the dawn of humankind and picture a human being laughing at another human being, tormenting him almost with this ridicule. Fast forward to the present day and this humiliation has crafted societies. Yes, we can make great strides, but we are also limited by the Labelling Phenomenon. We can only perceive reality in such a way.

Other animals can see, but cannot perceive the world as we do, because they lack language. A kangaroo is not afraid of being laughed at by another kangaroo. It cannot understand laughter. A kangaroo is not psychologically assaulted by the interpretation of another Kangaroo. Humans are assaulted by the interpretation of another human. Likewise, a blind person, much like a kangaroo, has no understanding of laughter, humiliation or shame, because they cannot see the faces of society.

We think we are determining the economic system. We think our behaviour determines the system. No, the system determines us, partly through the instrument of labelling.

We tie our self-esteem to being endorsed by the herd be it our friends, family or Facebook.

How much do men and women spend on trying to make themselves look desirable? The reason why 99.9% of men and women will die and be forgotten is that they measure success in being desired.

We instinctively label the hermetic individual who keeps to himself as odd. We instinctively label the person in love as normal. This has a powerful ramification on society. They wish to be labelled positively by the herd and how do they achieve this feat? Through being in a relationship. By being in a relationship, one neutralizes the Labelling Anxiety that is brought on by the Labelling Phenomenon.

We deliberately label the dysfunctional as outcasts. This in turn promotes conformism. People are too afraid to go alone. Schizoid PD for example is not really a personality disorder but can be thought of as a different mentality.

How many of society tie their happiness to image. When they look good, they in turn feel good. So, a man who earns a hundred grand a year, immediately feels content about such a proposition. And the woman who deems herself sexy, immediately feels good because she is attractive. Their happiness is contingent on depicting a positive image to the herd.

Theory of interpretation: The world will never be perfect as long as we interpret it. It is our interpretations that make the world positive or negative and not the world itself.

Out of our recklessness to control society we have given birth to criminality. Given man's inhumanity, the only means of eradicating crime is if you abolish the law.

"The looking glass self," was the term coined by sociologist Charles Horton Cooley. It expresses the tendency for one to understand oneself through their own understanding of the perception which others may hold of them. There are three main components that comprise the looking-glass self:

1. We imagine how we must appear to others.
2. We imagine and react to what we feel their judgment of that appearance must be.
3. We develop ourselves through the judgments of others.

The judiciary is a game of interpretation. It is one's interpretation versus another.

Everything is interpretation.

There are no laws; everything is permitted. But society has adopted a system of economic stability in favour of anarchy.

You are as much a potential perpetrator as you are a potential victim. It depends on how you are labelled.

The criminal is labelled. He is afraid to be recognised because of this label. But the law-abiding citizen is afraid also. He or she is afraid of being potentially labelled. The criminal is stigmatized; the law-abiding person is threatened with stigma. This threat of stigma is what I call the Labelling Anxiety. It follows us everywhere, so long as we interact with others. We behave in a way as to not be stigmatized (to not be negatively labelled.)

We are always striving to do the right thing given the situation or context. Let's say you see a person walking towards you that you know. The right thing in this situation is to say hello.

Every action carries the result of either a positive or negative label. Thus, what we try to do is carry out the action and be positively labelled at the same time.

The sociological fallout or by product of interaction is crime. When we interact with someone, that interaction is interpreted by the receiver. They either declare it to be positive or negative and if it is negative, we call that interaction a crime. Thus, it stands to reason that if you wish to limit crime, limit interaction. Yet the authorities would never dream of such an Orwellian world because we need people to interact so that the economic system can prevail.

It is our crimes that distinguish us. Without any convictions to our name, we are each and all identical.

Imagine the phenomenon when you walk down a street and recognise someone you know. If you analyse this interaction, you can learn so much. The second you recognise that person, your mind thinks to acknowledge them. So, you say "hello," and perhaps stop to chat to them. Why don't you just walk by them without acknowledging them? Why don't you do this with people you do not know? We want to be labelled positively; we strive often unconsciously to avoid a negative label. It gets interesting when you analyse Unconscious Labelling. Unconscious Labelling is where you are labelling those you do not even know. Such as people in a crowd at a rock concert. Now imagine that this labelling process is defective. It is malfunctioning. This is a part of schizophrenia I theorize. The way they label other people, whether they know them or not, is defective.

We are hypnotised by labels. Food, clothes and technology are the obvious ones. We need to buy specific brands to feel gratified. The less obvious ones are relationships and careers. This is the commoditization of our lives that consumes us. We need to be seen in a relationship and working a certain job just so we can be covertly approved by people we don't care about.

The Labelling Anxiety manipulates the individual at all times. "If I do this, how will I be labelled?" It is a phenomenon in both the individual and society. Being known warps the behaviour of the individual at all times. The individual responds to society. They respond to the potential threat of being negatively labelled. They walk up a street and do not run up one because of labelling, because of being known.

When we interact with society, we either positively label that interaction or negatively label it. Positive labelling is often unconscious, in that we do not realize we have positively labelled someone. Again, you walk up a street and do not run because you wish to be positively labelled by people you do not even know.

Labelling Anxiety: Imagine you are walking up a street with people walking in the opposite direction to you, as in they are walking against you. Now you do not know any of these people. Imagine now for instance three people who are walking against you stop, turn around and start running in the opposite direction they were originally walking. This is immediately labelled adversely by you. You then look behind you and see that a man is carrying a gun. But it is the fact that these people initially behaved in a way that you negatively labelled that caught your attention and these are people you do not know. The point I am trying to make is that even as you walk by people you do not know, you are all the time dividing their behaviour into Acceptable or Positive and Unacceptable or Negative. Again, a lot of this positive behaviour is only registered unconsciously. It is only when someone acts odd (negatively) that you register it consciously.

When you stand around waiting for a bus with other strangers, you may not know them but you are labelling them. Their behaviour is always divided into Acceptable or Unacceptable. As I assert, Acceptable behaviour is only registered by the unconscious. But should one member of that group behave erratically, he or she will become negatively labelled. For example, if one person took off all his or her clothes, he or she will be negatively labelled. But the important thing to remember is that they were positively labelled by everyone despite not being aware that they were labelled.

Being known is psychological assault on our mind. We do not perceive the assault, but we respond to it. So, when you are walking down the street and see someone you know, you instinctively think to say hello to them. Saying "hello" to them is the response to the assault. Likewise, when you walk down a busy city street and pass by people you do not know, you again respond to this assault by these people you do not know. So, you walk at a certain pace and avoid banging into these people. That is again how you respond to the assault you do not actually perceive. Now imagine this assault from being known is malfunctioning. How would it manifest itself? I theorize it would manifest itself by what we call schizophrenia. Schizophrenia in my opinion is just an adverse response to this psychological assault.

We fear a bear we meet in the woods. Likewise, we fear society, through them knowing us. Their interpretation of us is violence upon our conscience.

This assault, which is interpretation, which in actuality is how we are labelled, shapes or moulds society as much as desire or money or religion.

If stigma vanished, particularly the threat of stigma, this could destabilize society. The threat of stigma (the labelling anxiety) is vital for social cohesion.

We do not negatively label everyone, but we do threaten to negatively label everyone. This determines society. Then you have two responses to this threat of a negative label. One, is the mature response, in that you do not care what people think of you. You accept a negative label. Two, the immature response, where you conduct yourself in such a way to continuously avoid a negative label through obtaining a positive label.

The threat of stigma (The Labelling Anxiety) is everywhere. This threat of stigma is a huge component of the popularity of love.

I wonder if alien life from another star system or even galaxy would be able to distinguish between us. Would we all look the same and behave the same to them or would they like us humans do, distinguish between different types of people.

When people acknowledge us positively, we feel good. Thus, we tie our self-happiness to how we are labelled by those who perceive us.

Being known is both at once the venom and the mania of existence. When the people who know us approve of us, they make us feel worthy; but those who demean us, they make life unbearable.

The modern-day man and woman are under severe burden to be the modern-day man and woman. They are addicted to being labelled fittingly. This is why in part we chase relationships and professional careers. We want to be labelled positively by the herd, ergo our peers. This is most certainly the case with insecure people who are narcissistic.

You date not just because you just enjoy it but because you also gain pleasure from pacifying the herd. That you can convey to your peers that you are in a relationship makes you feel good.

We do so much in life just to be approved.

Existence is a crime; opinion is the punishment. We fear one's interpretation of us more than their fists.

We think we are living life to the fullest when all we are doing is carefully managing how society labels us. We want to live the dream life not because we independently choose to do so, but because we want to be approved by the herd. I see so many whose motivations for existence is approval.

Fame and criminality are the two extremes of being known.

We fear opinions more than guns. The criminal must fear bullets; the law-abiding individual must fear interpretation. Being known influences your behaviour. We are afraid of being known and we don't realize it, but we unconsciously respond to it.

Your life is what you interpret it to be.

Fame debases like no other. We are blind in the dark; but equally so we are blind when we stare at the sun.

Fame is as much a venom as it is an aphrodisiac. Success is often the failure.

Banking on fame making you happy is like jumping off a bridge and expecting to fly. Fame is a fickle friend.

A lot of anxiety stems from our peers, ergo those who know us. Now imagine you were famous, and your peers are the whole world. It explains why so many famous people commit suicide. They just cannot handle being known by everyone.

To be known by friends and family means we must acknowledge them or validate them. To be known by the whole world means we must authenticate the whole world.

An individual is either loved, despised or worst ignored.

I once heard a journalist say: "Real men don't visit prostitutes." In other words, they get married to achieve sexual fulfilment. But this is wrong. This version of men is from the perspective of the female majority and what they want the ideal man to do. It is like saying real women aren't overweight. This ideal woman that society idolizes is in turn the viewpoint of the male. We use the married man and woman as the template for society.

Women love a man in high demand which translates into they love a man that other women love. This is living-for-others rather than living-for-oneself.

Man is the only animal that can be shamed. This I feel is a component of schizophrenia.

Life is often a case of one's interpretation versus another's.

If you think of how fame corrupts and then apply that principle to the individual who is ordinary but has friends, co-workers, parents and a partner, you begin to understand the anxiety that torments man.

There is no such thing as a positive label because the very act of being labelled means that we become both controlled and condemned. Take a husband and wife for instance. The husband is labelled by the wife and must continue to fulfil obligations to remain a husband, as must the wife. They both must adjust their behaviour to accommodate the interpretation of the other.

There is a conflict between being known and desire. There also exists a conflict between being known and earning money. What I am trying to convey is that if you take sexual desire, a man for instance visits escorts to fulfil himself, but this desire exposes him to negative labelling. Likewise, with money, we need to work to earn a living, yet this working exposes us again to potential labelling from co-workers and bosses. Being known is existential suicide because we become afraid of the interpretation of those who know us.

Labelling is a unique element of being human. We do not label an animal a murderer or a genius. The animal is simply an animal responding to stimulus. With humans, we do label. In fact, every human we interact with is labelled. This labelling is the source of so much anxiety and woe. Very often the individual with low self-esteem yearns to be labelled more positively in life.

Society does not realize that the more they associate themselves within society the more damned they become.

Fame is a sort of paradox or contradiction, because we want to be famous for mass approval, but at the same time you have to live so carefully, almost like a hermit, to avoid these millions of people potentially negatively labelling you. It defeats its own purpose.

You don't really care about the welfare of your neighbour. But you deeply care about what this neighbour thinks of you. You care about his or her interpretation of you as they see you.

Where society is, the threat of stigma is. You cannot have one without the other. Within society, stigma is not everywhere, but the threat of stigma is everywhere.

A neurotic person fears being negatively labelled. What we define a healthy individual is one that is seduced by the chance of accruing a positive label. For example, the neurotic fears the next day at work because he or she fears doing something wrong and hence becomes negatively labelled. The healthy individual in contrast looks forward to getting a new job because he or she sees it as something they can build their life on. They are seduced by the reward of a positive label.

The healthy individual is so conditioned to man that they don't see him as a menace.

If we all wore masks, life would be much simpler. Suicide is being known.

Anonymity is freedom.

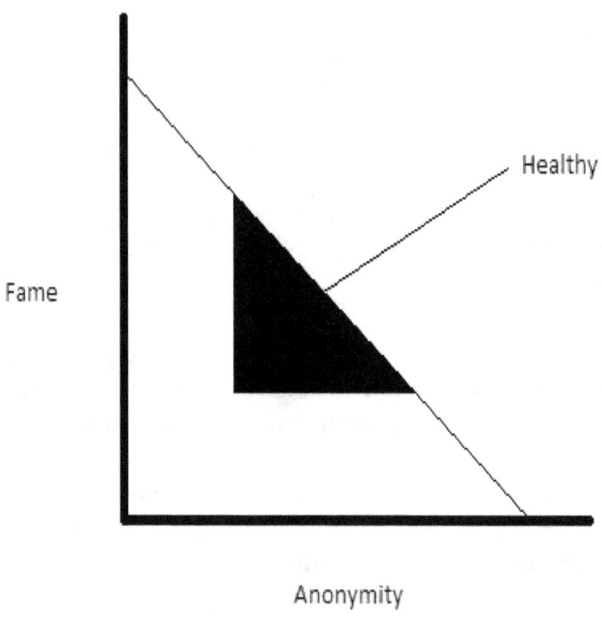

Fig 1: *Too much fame and too much anonymity can be detrimental to one's mental health.*

"I knew a man who was blind. When he was nearly 40 years old he had an operation and regained his sight.... At first he was elated, really high—faces, colours, landscapes. But then everything began to change. The world was much poorer than he had imagined. No one had ever told him how much dirt there was, how much ugliness. He noticed ugliness everywhere. When he was blind, he used to cross the street alone with a stick. After he regained his sight, he became afraid, he began to live in darkness, he never left his room. After three years he killed himself." - The Passenger (A film by Michelangelo Antonioni).

We are dictating each other's behaviour and we do not realize it. We do not want to be negatively labelled and thus try to appease the other individual(s). This applies to a relationship or society overall.

The only way one can be absolutely free is to not be known because when they are not known they are not labelled. Alas the economic system kills this. Within the current economic system, we are compelled to socialize.

If you analyse suicide amongst people, I would wager that being negatively labelled had a huge bearing in the suicide. Perhaps the individual fell out with friends or a lover; perhaps the individual kept viewing his or herself as a failure. Those are simply different ways of saying they are negatively labelled and wish to be positively labelled.

We live in a labelling culture. The Labelling Phenomenon is one of the reasons we are distracted from the universe. When you interact with people, regardless of whether you know them or not, you are so preoccupied with labelling that you do not have time to think otherwise. Apply this to friendship, to work, to walking up a busy city street by yourself. In all three of those things, you seldom think about the nature of the universe or the complexity of the atom. All three things have distracted you, through (in part) the Labelling Anxiety. You are so preoccupied with managing your interaction with these people, that the true nature of the world is a distant thought.

You have what I term the 95/5 percent rule. Only 5 people out of a 100 have the courage to be disliked in society. On the other hand, 95% of people are very socially conscious. They try to be approved or maintain approval at all times.

What is your motivation? Why do you do what you do? Why do you want what you want? Specifically, you want to turn up at your school reunion after thirty years and for everyone to look at you and say: "I wish I had the life he has."

Driven by labels, the thought of not being deemed good enough torments the individual. If they fancy someone in their immediate life and subsequently get turned down by that person, they then feel inadequate and this irritates them. Not being liked is a diminutive form of ostracization that hurts us deeply.

"The condition of alienation, of being asleep, of being unconscious, of being out of one's mind, is the condition of the normal man. Society highly values its normal man. It educates children to lose themselves and to become absurd, and thus to be normal. Normal men have killed perhaps 100,000,000 of their fellow normal men in the last fifty years." - R.D. Laing

Your enthusiasm to be labelled positively is just another way of saying you fear being labelled negatively.

Your freedom involves many things. One of the essential needs is that you outgrow this Labelling Anxiety. Unfortunately, most people don't mature out of the phase until they grow old. The trick is to be mature as an adult when you are young.

You may conclude that when you walk up a busy city street or sit in a lecture theatre in college, that you are just ignoring all the people around you, whether you know them or not. The reality is that you do acknowledge them. You are labelling their behaviour at all times, as they are you. Basically, you are afraid of them, you are afraid of being negatively labelled by them, you are afraid of being laughed at by them, but it is often unconscious. This is why in part you conform, because it is a means to neutralize the threat of being adversely labelled. That is the Labelling Anxiety. This is why you behave a precise way because you know this is how society will positively label you. Now two things to ponder: A) You are not afraid of what animals think of you, only humans. You may fear a bear in that it may attack you, but you are not afraid of being laughed at by that said bear. This is a trait that exists solely in humans because we can use language to label in another way. B) What if this whole process by which you label and are labelled is malfunctioning? What if it was defective? This is why I theorize that labelling is a part of schizophrenia.

Imagine sitting in a coffee shop minding your own business and there are other people doing the same, people you do not know. You are interacting with them because you are labelling how they behave, often unconsciously. So long as they all keep to themselves, you pay no attention to them, as in you unconsciously label their behaviour as appropriate. But if one person started shouting in a negative manner, you would then consciously label that behaviour and hence person as inappropriate.

You cannot have a society without the labelling phenomenon and hence labelling anxiety/threat of stigma. Once you interact with people, regardless of whether you know them or not, you are unconsciously always striving to do the correct thing given the context. This threat of stigma moulds society. It dictates how we behave.

Exposure to the herd is a psychological assault upon your identity. This is part of how you are manipulated into instinctively thinking about being in a relationship. Now you do not perceive the assault and nor do you often perceive the response. You just instinctively react to this assault by thinking of behaving a certain way, in order to be approved. Socialization, something which is seen as the foundation of human existence, actually works against us, in that it gives rise to insecurity.

The more we expose ourselves to the herd, the more we are compelled to adopt the herds ideology. Exposure manipulates your decision process. Why does everyone think of being in a relationship? They do in part because of this exposure to the herd. Be it education or work, when we embroil ourselves with other people, we seek to be labelled positively by them and to do this we need to be in a relationship. There is a link between being sociable and wanting to be in a relationship. Socialization enforces a relationship upon you.

When using an anonymous alias on an internet forum we fear our real identity being discovered. Now one must apply that fear to the real world of interaction. When we interact with people, we at all times fear their interpretation of us. We thus try to be endorsed by them and they by us. They control our behaviour and we in turn control theirs. When they approve of us, we feel good, but when they dismiss us, we feel bad. It stands to reason that if one truly wishes to be free, they would be advised to live alone and avoid everyone. In living in seclusion, they cannot be interpreted and hence controlled. Furthermore, they do not rely on others approval to be of esteem.

To rid the world of evil, rid the world of man, because without man and man's interpretation there is no geniuses or monsters, no good or bad. The animal cannot interpret and that is why there is no evil in the animal kingdom.

Is the world imperfect because people do evil things or is it because we can interpret those evil doings as evil? There are no criminals in the animal kingdom. The foundations of good and bad are at the behest of man's interpretation.

As long as you are different you will be labelled.

We are obsessed with being labelled appropriately through obtaining the correct labels or a precise image. A man needs the correct watch, the correct clothes, the correct hairstyle, the correct car and not surprisingly the correct woman. He treats his partner as a mechanism of which to gain a distinguished label. This is not love; this is a commoditized relationship. Now the female of society does the same thing. Why do some females crave the man in high demand? They do so because when they are seen attached to one, they get labelled positively by their peers. Labelling (the reward of a positive label) has such a huge psychological influence on our decision making. If the individual improves our image (how we are labelled by the herd) we have a good chance of choosing the individual to be our partner.

You understand the power of labelling when someone commits a crime. What you do not see is the power of labelling done by friends, family and co-workers. You adjust your behaviour to appease these people.

Society and stigma are intertwined. They are the two sides of the same coin. You cannot have society without stigma, and likewise if there is stigma, its source is society.

Marrying someone for a good label is nothing more than a marriage of convenience.

A nuclear holocaust or a chemical warfare is not our biggest fear. Our biggest fear is that people will not like us. Thus, our daily existence is plagued with this fear and hence we do so much to try and get people to approve of us.

We are at all times unconsciously saying to ourselves: If I am seen with this (be it a person or a house or a piece of clothing), how will the herd interpret me? Your mind is frequently asking this question. What it conveys is that ultimately you are afraid of what people think of you and as such try to engineer your projection in such a way that you are validated.

It is a very fragile world we inhabit because we are constantly being bombarded by one's interpretation of us. We are always trying to maintain a positive label.

Laughter is often the sculptor of society.

The price you pay every day for being validated is you must validate others in return. We are at once both the conditioner and conditioned of society. The reason in part why you don't commit crime is the same reason in part why you get married and have two children, and is the same reason why you travel fifty miles just to shake a colleague's hand at a funeral for two seconds. In all those things you are carefully managing how society labels you.

Stigma is a vital cog in the cogwheel that is society. Stigma is not necessarily good for the individual, but it is enormously beneficial for society. It is because we strive to live in such a way as to avoid stigma. The obvious example is we avoid being a criminal. The less obvious example is we get married and have two children, again to avoid stigma. The same stigma that commentators say we should end, is the very same stigma that binds society.

Once known you are labelled and cruelly damned. Sartre said man is condemned to choose. The by-product of choice is being labelled. Thus, man is condemned to be labelled.

Ross Lockridge Jr who wrote a best seller in Raintree County (and became famous) committed suicide due to the pressures of fame. He committed suicide due to the pressure of being known. "I walk past people," he confided to his wife, "and I wonder what they think." Being labelled is the sum of all our fears. But we are in a bind in that we are forced to advertise our identity to the herd. So, what we instinctively do to neutralize this angst is conform.

It is well known that Truman Capote's greatest achievement and greatest failure was his book In Cold Blood. The success of that book ultimately killed him. Fame is most certainly not the solution to your problems. More tears are shed over answered prayers than unanswered ones.

I remember reading an article about a man who won the lotto and he said it destroyed him and that he wished he had never won it. He said that because of his fame after winning it, people started looking for money and suing him. Again, this provides more fuel to my theory that being known is not a luxury, but a hindrance.

Opinion is akin to a biological virus, spreading from host to host, mutating in that time. The only method of preventing the virus from spreading is to not be known.

Life is not life; society is life. We are products of our culture and not of the universe.

We are caught in the midst of a sociological snowstorm; a battle between exposure and acceptance. Stigma is vital for societies because stigma leads to competition. People try to outdo their peers, as to who has the best life. They seek adoration to counter the stigma.

Removing stigma from society would have the same effect as removing gravity from the physics of the universe. As in society would cease to function.

Immersed within society we are engaged in a never-ending psychological warfare. A sociological game theory. We must be validated by those that know us and consequently we must in turn validate them. If the two people validate each other the equilibrium remains intact.

Why doesn't the female of society cut her hair short? What is motivating the hordes of women to conform to have long hair? Well look at it like this: What happens if a woman decides to have short hair? She gets labelled negatively by her peers. Her parents, her friends and her co-workers will speak negatively about her. She will no longer be deemed attractive to the male of society. This negative labelling is just another way of saying she is afraid of what people think of her. Thus, to be free in an existential method is to dissolve this fear. It is to approach life in a released method. Aim to be an existential criminal but within the law.

No reputation is better than a bad reputation. To be unknown is better than to be convicted.

Through labelling society regulates the individual which in turn regulates society itself.

Conformity, narcissism and schizophrenia are in ways, three different responses to being known, to being labelled.

Forgiveness, do not make me laugh, once known, you can never be forgiven.

The battlefield is the streets of the secure western society; the battleground is the hearts of the moralistic.

You rarely see a famous woman having one-night stands. Famous men, yes, but famous women, no. Why the difference? The answer is stigma. The media will report on these famous women in a negative light if they do have one-night stands.

Look at the famous person. They are hounded by the media. This also applies to the average person. Who are they hounded by? They are by their peerage.

Now I see no resolution to this dilemma or insecurity. Such is the economic system that we are born to parents, then educated, and then must work, and these three things control our behaviour and hence make us conform because they make us insecure. But do not doubt me when I say that if you can distance yourself from these three things, you can become much more secure and hence happy in your existence. But given the current economic system, being emotionally secure and being financially secure are often mutually exclusive.

One's infatuation with success, wealth, looking attractive, starting a family, is just a product of socialization. They are a derivative of exposure to society.

Man can be everything except nothing.

Schizoid and Avoidant are both influenced by the threat of being labelled. The avoidant fears being negatively labelled. For example, they fear being called ugly or short or fat or unintelligent and so on. The schizoid on the other hand is not afraid of being slandered so to speak. The schizoid fears exposure of his identity to the other. It is more of an existential threat.

Given the current economic system, interaction is a necessity, but this interaction is a source of angst for the individual. So how do we negotiate this anxiety? We use the myth of true love to neutralize the anxiety in being in a relationship with someone. That we can love and be loved overwhelms the anxiety of being known. With work we use the reward of money to counter the threat of being known. Earning money pulverises this existential threat. Both love and money are a means to seduce the individual so that they will adopt the system.

A large part of the reason why we have so many conformists and so few rebels is that people are rattled. They are afraid to go alone through this world. They are afraid of what their parents, friends and co-workers will say about them.

We are condemned to choose and henceforth condemned to be labelled. The only way you cannot be labelled is if you cannot choose and the only way you can't choose is if you are not alive.

You must remember that in today's world even the person you love has the potential to be a journalist.

Collective interpretation is what controls society.

The battle of minorities is a battle of labelling. They fight to be positively labelled. The crisis of failure is often a crisis of labelling.

My advice is do the opposite to what the system has taught you. From a young age you are taught to interact and to expose your identity to people. My philosophy is to limit this exposure. Limit how many people know you and become happy in the silence.

Through labelling and the threat of a potential negative label, society reaches a sort of equilibrium. You can see the equilibrium when walking in a busy city street. Everyone makes adjustments to not bump into each other. Everyone walks up the street and does not run. They cross the road when it is clear to do so. Labelling is shaping how they behave. Of course, when something negative happens, it disrupts this equilibrium. If for example a car crashes into a pedestrian, we negatively label that event. Or if someone took off all their clothes or attacked someone, again the equilibrium is disrupted.

When the equilibrium is disturbed, we send the guilty party off to prisons, psychiatric hospitals, we write about them in the papers, we laugh at them and we stigmatize them.

Labelling Equilibrium. We behave in such a way to maintain the equilibrium. In a coffee shop for example, everyone behaves in such a way to maintain the equilibrium, to maintain a positive label. They wait for their latte or they sit chatting to friends, they say "thank you" to the barista and so on. They are all the time adjusting their behaviour to maintain a positive label, to maintain the equilibrium.

Conformity is a by-product of the Labelling Anxiety and hence Labelling Phenomenon. Conformity is how we instinctively respond to society and society's interpretation. It is how we maintain our positive label, and in our quest to maintain such a positive label we hence maintain the equilibrium.

The man is addicted to sex; the woman, to being labelled in love.

The existential paradox is this: It is the people you love who you actually fear.

A relationship by default gives birth to the Labelling Anxiety and hence the Labelling Bind. Both the male and female (or perhaps two males/females) become anxious at the thought of losing the relationship. This is the Labelling Anxiety. To neutralize this anxiety, they conform to their partners wishes. This is the Labelling Bind. An obvious example is the female fears her husband not finding her attractive anymore (Labelling Anxiety) and so must continue to try to remain as attractive as possible (Labelling Bind). Likewise, the husband must continue to work to earn money so his wife will stay with him. The same mechanism can be applied to friendship or work relations. We all the time must behave a certain way to maintain a positive label.

To genuinely love you must violate the tribe.

Take the famous person for instance. That they are exposing their identity to the greater society, like a film star for instance, they then must adjust their behaviour so that they are positively labelled by society. They are not deciding how they behave. Society is deciding for them, without them being cognizant of this regulation. This is why so many escorts must hide their identities, because they are defying this regulation and hence become negatively labelled as a result. The other thing is that you can apply this same regulation of the famous person to the non-famous person. In such a case they are regulated by their peerage. There is truly little difference in terms of the dynamics between global fame and the classroom.

You cannot separate society from the sane. The number of women casually walking into plastic surgery offices, asking the consultant for the "Kylie Jenner look" is a result of socialization. Such insecure women are doing it because that is a product of their regulation by society.

The line between lionization and derision is extremely thin, to the point that few realize it when they have crossed it.

Remove society and you remove the narcissism, the insecurity, the anguish, the overwhelming desire to be happier than others and so on.

We become what we repeatedly see.

The urge to avoid being stigmatized within society only leads to the threat of being stigmatized by that very same society.

If I sexually assaulted someone I knew, they would negatively label me and rightly so. Now let's analyse another interaction. Let us say I see them walking down the street and they say hello to me, but I just walk on by without replying. What do they think of me then? They negatively label me again. Can you see what I am trying to suggest: both interactions lead to a negative label. Being impolite to someone results in the same label as sexually assaulting them. Fear drives us. In the same way that we try to avoid committing crime against someone, we also strive to prevent them from thinking that we are rude to them.

The insecure are so addicted to being labelled appropriately that it confines them to immaturity. Their whole journey of existence becomes one of labelling gratification and not one of sincere enjoyment. They marry, they work, they conduct themselves all so they can be positively labelled by their peerage. To escape this wrath of labelling is to mature.

Imagine how uncomfortable it would be if everyone knew each other. Imagine for instance walking down a street and you recognise everyone, and they recognise you; you would almost feel like a criminal in such a situation. This is the threat of being known. Thus, there are two states: One in which we are known and one in which we are anonymous, and you need a bit of both to be secure. But too much of any one state can be detrimental.

To be existentially mature you must rid yourself of this Labelling Anxiety.

To be known is to be condemned and to be condemned is to be known. You can only label someone if you know them. The more known you are, the more you risk being labelled.

Why on the internet do escorts hide their faces and married women do not? When you understand that proposition you can understand labels.

Recognition is an event horizon that cannot be reversed. Once known, you are condemned.

You should never hate who you are; you should hate what society tells you to be. Society has created you; maturity is creating yourself.

In the concentration camp, we fear the guards; in the totalitarian regime, we fear the government; in the free world, we fear the people we know, the people we love.

We exist, we expose ourselves to the herd, they then interpret us, this creates anxiety.

Our greatest hopes and worst fears lie in being labelled. How people interpret us has a huge bearing on how happy we are.

Many people remark about how they would hate to be famous. To have that level of scrutiny within your life would be nothing short of suicide. Now you must apply that same fear and apprehension to the non-famous or normal individual. In this case, you fear the people who know you. You fear your friends; they mould you. You fear your co-workers; they shape you. You fear the people you recognise when you walk down the street; they decide you. If we were famous, we would acknowledge the anxiety consciously. With the normal person, this anxiety is unconscious.

There is a conflict raging in the minds of men: The system says expose yourself, but this exposure means one can become adversely labelled.

One of the by-products of forcing society together is everyone becomes afraid of gossip and strives to avoid it at all costs. To avoid this stigma, they pursue a hedonistic lifestyle and try to look happier than all their peers.

Life is often a battle between desire and being labelled.

Desire vs labelling. We desire sex but can be negatively labelled as a result. We desire money but can be negatively labelled through work problems.

The Labelling Conflict: You desire things in life, but this desire exposes you to interpretation from the individual or herd. You need sexual fulfilment but become subordinate to the person you have sexual relations with. You need money to survive but become a slave to how your co-workers interpret you.

Labelling Conflict: Men and women to a degree are so afraid of being labelled negatively. For instance, they are afraid of being labelled a "virgin." That causes them to seek sex, and they can become adversely labelled as a result. We want to live but this living often conflicts with interpretation.

People's behaviour on anonymous forums on the internet differs from their behaviour in the real world. Why is this? It is because in the real world they are exposing their full identity to the observing herd and this manipulates how they behave.

All the conforming class have is their interpretation, but it stings like no other.

Human beings lost a part of their soul when we first learned how to laugh.

Labelling Bind. You meet friends, they invite you out and because you don't wish to offend them, you agree. This "going out" then exposes you to more and more people, which you come to fear, which in turn can expose you to even more people. This is the Labelling Chain Reaction. It is a chain reaction. You are afraid of a negative label, which dictates your behaviour, which in turn leads you to be labelled even more.

Labelling Chain Reaction: Think of the nuclear fission chain reaction. One neutron releases two neutrons, those two neutrons release four neutrons and so on. That is what knowing people does. One person that knows you means more people will know you. That you are afraid of being labelled adversely by one person means you become labelled by other people just to pacify (avoid a negative label) the original person who knows you.

Money exposes us to interpretation; desire exposes us to interpretation; then interpretation exposes us to more interpretation. In the battle between desire, money and interpretation, the outcome is conformity.

Imagine you know Person A (PA) at work. (PA) invites you out for drinks on a Friday. You don't actually want to go, but you know (PA) will be disappointed (Labelling Anxiety) in you should you not go. So, you accept his offer. You agree to meet up (Labelling Bind.) When out having a drink (PA) introduces you to another person, Person B (PB). So, you have gone from knowing one person to knowing two. Now, on another day, you are minding your own business doing shopping in the shopping store and you see (PB), who is with his different friend Person C (PC). You stop and chat to (PB) who then introduces you to (PC). Now you know three people: (PA), (PB) and (PC). So the initial fear of being negatively labelled (Labelling Anxiety) by (PA), which in turn made you socialize (Labelling Bind) and has now made you be known by two more people (PB) and (PC) (Labelling Chain Reaction). This is the Labelling Chain Reaction brought on by the Labelling Bind brought on by the Labelling Anxiety.

The irony of labels is that we fear being labelled a loner or odd and hence socialize with other people and hence become afraid of being negatively labelled by them. The immature individual is in a catch-22. They do not wish to be labelled a social recluse, but they also do not wish to be negatively labelled (gossiped) by another. The urge not to be labelled odd is much greater than the fear of being negatively labelled by someone they know. Thus, they broadcast themselves to the greater population and become controlled. This game haunts them to the day they die.

Threatened With Labels ———— Conforms ———— Becomes Labelled

Fig 2: *Man is condemned to be labelled.*

We exist and are threatened with being negatively labelled should we not conform (not adhere to the economic system). This is the Labelling Bind. To neutralize this threat, we conform, but in doing so we become labelled and hence controlled. A prime example of this is marriage. It is imposed on the individual but then they become subordinate to their partner's interpretation of them and vice versa (The Labelling Anxiety). They then must meet friends and family of their partner (The Labelling Bind), exposing their identity to even more people and thus becoming afraid of being labelled negatively by these other people (Labelling Chain Reaction).

So basically, the individual is caught either way. They live in solitude and thus become negatively labelled or they conform in which case they are fearful of a negative label and sometimes actually become negatively labelled. The marriage could fail, or they could lose friends in which the positive adoration morphs into negative opinion.

Social media is a prime example of the Labelling Bind and Labelling Chain Reaction. If we choose not to be on social media, we get negatively labelled and thus this threat motivates us to be on social media to avoid a negative label. The Labelling Anxiety makes us fear being labelled negatively, so we go on social media to be part of the crowd (The Labelling Bind). But by being on social media, we get labelled anyway as we expose our identity to even more people and must behave a certain way in order to be approved (The Labelling Chain Reaction).

The Labelling Anxiety and Labelling Bind: Imagine a friend asks you to meet for coffee. You say no because you are busy. That same friend asks you one month later the same question, to meet for coffee. Again, you say no for a certain reason. The same friend asks you again, a month later, to meet for coffee. Now you are thinking that if you reject them again, they will be disappointed in you (negatively label you). So now, at the third time of asking, you meet up. The threat of a negative label (Labelling Anxiety) has decided how you behave (Labelling Bind.) The Labelling Bind demonstrates the anxiety with being known. A friend or perhaps a partner asks you to do something you do not wish to do. But you end up doing it anyway, despite your reluctance because you know that if you do not do it, you will be labelled negatively by the said friend or partner. The moral is as Schopenhauer alluded to that being known leads to angst. So, if you minimize being known (as hard as it is to do in the present world) you can become happier.

The positives of labelling are morality and compassion. The negatives are insecurity and narcissism.

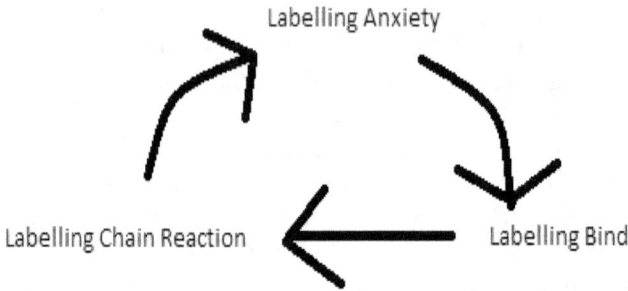

Labelling Anxiety

Labelling Chain Reaction

Labelling Bind

Fig 3: *The Labelling Anxiety gives birth to the Labelling Bind, which in turn gives birth to the Labelling Chain Reaction and so the cycle continues.*

Being known is a psychological rape upon our identity. But in a world where socialization is seen as the norm, our minds must adapt to take this existential onslaught. They do so through conforming. By conforming one can socialize and be secure in knowing that they will be labelled correctly.

You are not afraid of being laughed at by a dog or a cat. But you are afraid of being laughed at by another human being. You are not afraid of a negative label from a dog or a cat. But you are afraid of a negative label from another human being. Being known by a human is vastly different from being known by any other animal. So how do we negate this fear of being laughed at by other humans? Simple, we conform.

Who is more affected by the threat of gossip or even actual gossip itself, the male or the female? I have my suspicions it is the female, which is beneficial for society, because it means they are more afraid of going against the current than men.

Once known, man is stalked, incarcerated, condemned and existentially guillotined. It is most dangerous to be known.

People are more likely when on anonymous forums to be rude or condescending. Whereas in real life they would not behave as such. What that says is that when we are known, we tend to adjust our behaviour to be positively labelled.

We are slaves to money, desire and interpretation. Unconsciously these three things are deciding our behaviour. Imagine you are at work and get the urge to buy a cup of coffee. First is the desire to have it, that motivates you. Then you must check you have enough money to buy it. In order to have money you must work for it. Then you must get permission to leave your workplace to buy it. You must be positively interpreted by your boss or co-workers.

Labelling is the glue that binds society together.

"The condition of man... is a condition of war of everyone against everyone." – Thomas Hobbes

Being known by a human being is vastly different than being known by any other animal. If you were walking down the street and saw a dog and said hello to him, he will not say hello back. But you do not care one bit. You are not expecting him to say hello back because he is a dog. Now replace that dog with someone you know. You say hello and they just ignore you. How do you feel then? You think this person does not like you anymore or perhaps you did something to offend them.

Stigma (Labelling Anxiety) moulds societies. The threat of being stigmatized determines how one thinks and acts. We think only the criminal is stigmatized. But the normal citizen is also moulded by this very same stigma. The result is different though. The criminal covers his face and changes his identity. The normal person seeks to conform.

Our relationships with others are fragile things, almost on the knife's edge. They can end like the flick of a switch. We can shun others or be shunned by others, for very little it must be said.

Émile Durkheim famously argued that crime was a part of social cohesion. Crime plays a role in stabilizing society. We watch the news or read the papers and we see how the criminals behave and this then in turn tells us how to behave and how not to behave within society. The same can be applied to the threat of stigma, in that firstly, it is vital for social cohesion, and secondly, through hearing about how others are stigmatized, laughed at, demeaned and so forth, we learn how to behave so that we in turn will not be stigmatized, laughed at and demeaned.

The latent homosexual fears being "outed." That is the threat of stigma.

Stigma only comes into play when you are amongst other people. Regardless of whether you know them or not. This is the labelling equilibrium which is maintained as long as we are labelled positively and label others positively. If you think of space time and apply a similar method to stigma. For example, if you walked up a busy shopping centre, filled with thousands of people. All these people are labelling each other. All are thus striving to do the correct thing to maintain the labelling equilibrium.

The labelling phenomenon is a field much like space time is to general relativity. But this field requires more than one person to be in proximity to each other. Imagine someone all alone in their house with the curtains drawn. They may behave differently than they would if someone else was with them in the said house. So, they may talk to themselves or go to the toilet with the door open, things they would not dream of doing if they were amongst another person.

We are controlled by money, desire and interpretation. Money is economics; desire is evolutionary; interpretation is sociological. The system requires that we work; then we need to eat and have sex; finally, we become a slave to those who know us.

We cannot see the oppression. We cannot see the bind of being known. If we err in life the neighbours will not like us. Likewise, if we walk by our neighbours without saying hello, they will not like us either.

Not being polite gives birth to the same negative label from someone, as if one were a convicted sex offender.

The insecure suffer an intense Labelling Anxiety.

Society mistakes being labelled positively for not being labelled at all.

Being known promotes social control. Interpretation (labelling) controls society.

You cannot understand schizophrenia without understanding the Labelling Phenomenon.

We like being flattered only because we know that being humiliated is a horrible sensation. How do we become flattered? How do we earn approval? By conforming. We must be beautiful, rich, insanely happy and furthermore we must show everyone.

You cannot speak about the individual without including society. People are seldom alone in this world, until they die. They are adulterated by the society they grow up in. A great deal of who they are is thus owed to society. They are a society of individuals and not individuals of society.

You have two types of people within society: the stigmatized and those threatened by stigma. Those that are stigmatized display to those threatened by stigma how to behave.

You can run from your demons, but only if they are not you. You cannot escape yourself. Akin to the textbook schizoid, such a person always thinks, if not dreams, that if only they could start again somewhere new and different, then they could attain a better life. But where you go, your life goes with you.

So much of yourself owes itself to society. Our dreams, our attributes, our faults and insecurities, more likely than not are societal. "Not a very sharp line can be drawn between social psychology and individual psychology." - George Herbert Mead.

There is a culture of racism, prejudice and stigma. Unless you are white, healthy, heterosexual and married with two kids, you are generally afflicted by those three things.

Because of labelling there is always a sort of conflict or battle raging when we interact with others. We expect to be validated by other people, but we in turn must validate them.

You see commentators remarking that there is a culture of racism against people who are black, or gay, or trans etc. They are not wrong. I am not trying to side with the left, but the only person who is immune from stigma in life is the white healthy heterosexual male who is married with two children. Even those single men who choose not to follow such a path are stigmatized.

The devoted partner of exposure is presentation management.

If you end the stigma against escorts for example, you thereby end the same stigma that forces men and women to get married and have two children. That would be detrimental for society. One could suggest or argue that the fact that we stigmatize the mentally ill or the escorts or the homosexuals, shows that society is healthy. Stigma is a vital cog in society's sustainability.

That capitalistic society is inherently narcissistic, socialization does more damage to the individual than good. In contrast, socialization in poor countries is beneficial. So really if you want to mature in western societies, you have to minimize socialization.

It is very difficult for the individual to change themselves. Usually they only change if the culture they live in changes. No individual can change society; it takes society to change society.

Modern society is basically Economic Stockholm Syndrome on a mass scale.

It takes existentially immature people to sustain the system, people who only see life as a work and love. If they were philosophically smart, they would see the universe and hence be less likely to have children.

The threat of stigma (the labelling anxiety) moulds our appearance, our behaviour, our dreams, and our happiness or unhappiness.

"What kind of men, then, does our society need? What is the "social character" suited to twentieth century Capitalism? It needs men who co-operate smoothly in large groups; who want to consume more and more, and whose tasks are standardized and can easily be influenced and anticipated. It needs men who feel free and independent, not subject to any authority, or principle, or conscience - yet willing to be commanded, to do what is expected, to fit into the social machine without friction." - Erich Fromm

We only worry about physical violence from another person when faced with it. In contrast, we unconsciously fear being labelled by society every second of every day of every year. This is the ultimate fear of mankind: Being labelled by another person or persons.

If you take two people who meet each other by chance on the city street. Both must acknowledge each other (say hello) in order to be approved by each other. There exists a sort of game theory conflict between both of them. Now you could apply this to two (or more) people who do not know each other but interact, such as walking by each other on a city street.

Person A

	Does not say hello	Says hello
Person B Does not say hello	X	X
Says hello	X	O

Fig 4: *Conflict (a negative label) arises on three occasions. Only when the two people both behave positively to each other, is conflict avoided.*

Interaction between humans actually blinds us to the universe. We are distracted from the true realities of the world through the very fact that we socialize with each other. We are so consumed with how we are labelled that we negate the atom and the miracle of the universe

Everything is being interpreted. Every interaction is being scrutinized. Every time you meet someone be it ordering a cup of coffee or talking to a friend, your unconscious mind is making decisions. "Is that appropriate or inappropriate?" "Is it acceptable or unacceptable?"

If we were all blind, life paradoxically, would be much simpler. We would not be worried by what people thought of us. We would not fear their labels.

You will not value your anonymity in life unless you err.

Stigma is a subtle threat to everyone else. If you behave the same as the ostracized individual, then you will be ostracized yourself.

Society is far too complex to ever be fully understood.

Simply exposing yourself to society influences your life choices.

Think of two people who work together. When they meet in the street or in the office in the morning, they greet each other. Now look at what happens when one person does not greet the other. They fall out. Essentially everyone's behaviour is controlled by the other individual. This behaviour of greeting people is decided by the fact that they know each other. Another way to think of it is that imagine these people had never known each other and let us say they pass by each other on a busy city street. They just walk by each other and never see each other again. That they do not know each other means they cannot be controlled by each other. What I am trying to convey is that one's behaviour is decided by the people who know you.

For the narcissistically inclined, altering their life is understood to be altering people's opinion of them.

Another way to understand the threat of stigma (the labelling anxiety) is to understand reputation and the loss of it that someone experiences when they do something deviant. Thus, the individual, conscious of this, conscious of how the homosexuals or the escorts or the mentally ill or the sex offenders are degraded, makes his or her choices in such a way to maintain a positive reputation (a positive label.) Attempting to accrue a positive reputation or retain it, which manifests itself in trying to live the dream life, is actually the urge to avoid stigma (a negative label.)

Stigmatizing others is in ways a self-stigmatization. It is because you come to understand that you do not wish to be stigmatized as those you are stigmatizing. For example, if you gossip about someone in some way, you at the same time conduct yourself in such a way that you will not be subjected to the same gossip.

They say women are fiercely competitive with regards to picking a partner. What competitive means is they are fixated with how they are labelled by society with regards to who they choose. Being competitive in life means you are very conscious of how the herd labels you.

It is not the plastic surgeon that moulds our bodies, but opinion. Opinion is the silent sculptor of society.

Capitalism is driven, in part, by the selection of the sexes. It is driven, in part, by labels. Men select women who are physically attractive. But women select men who are successful.

For standing up against society, for being who you are, for not being a puppet people pleaser, the price you will pay is ostracization. It takes the courage to be disliked to be a strong person.

There is no derogatory term for the married heterosexul, with two kids, a good job, a nice house and a nice car. That is why everyone chases such a life, because it is not stigmatized.

Society is violence. It cannot function otherwise. It takes laughter, ridicule, humiliation and stigma to make society function. Modern human society is its own Serengeti.

It is a society of threats. If you cheat on your partner, if you don't go to a party you were invited to, if you commit a crime, and so on, you will be ostracized by society.

It is not fame that is killing reality tv stars in their droves. It is in fact society that is killing them.

The worst thing you can do to someone is not to hate them, but to not care about them. By not caring about someone, you are essentially saying that you don't care that they won't like you, for not caring about them.

Once thrown into the lions-pit that is society, laudation becomes the only way to tame the beasts. Granted, most will not understand, unless they err in life, but opinion is the price we pay for our genius.

That we are labelling others, means we understand that we are labelled ourselves by others. This endeavours to make us very status conscious. The competitive nature of society we live in, is the result of labelling.

You hear commentators remarking how the tabloids and journalists have no ethics or morality, in that they will print a story for the headlines and ruin lives. But these tabloids do play an especially important role as Émile Durkheim would testify to. The tabloids show the normal law-abiding citizens how to behave within society. We read the tabloids and we adjust our behaviour so that we will hopefully never be written about in the tabloids themselves. As in if you banish the tabloids and all forms of journalism to aid society, to protect people, that will only lead to an increase in deviance. People need, in order to be good, the bad to compare themselves and their behaviour to. To paraphrase Gore Vidal, someone must err for you to prosper.

We are born free. Then parents label us. Then we are educated and labelled by our friends. We then must work and become labelled by our co-workers. These three entities (parents; friends; co-workers) all determine our wills and wants purely because they can label us.

"The conscious and intelligent manipulation of the organized habits and opinions of the masses is an important element in democratic society. Those who manipulate this unseen mechanism of society constitute an invisible government which is the true ruling power of our country. ...We are governed, our minds are molded, our tastes formed, our ideas suggested, largely by men we have never heard of. This is a logical result of the way in which our democratic society is organized. Vast numbers of human beings must cooperate in this manner if they are to live together as a smoothly functioning society. ...In almost every act of our daily lives, whether in the sphere of politics or business, in our social conduct or our ethical thinking, we are dominated by the relatively small number of persons...who understand the mental processes and social patterns of the masses. It is they who pull the wires which control the public mind." - Edward Bernays

By removing stigma, you remove the threat of stigma, which is something that stabilizes society.

I remember reading on a forum, a question that was put to the female subscribers of that forum: if you knew a man that visited escorts, would you date that man? The vast majority of female posters said that they would not go near such a man. This is the threat that women put towards men. "If you don't behave in such a way, then we will not like you." It is essentially a threat of stigma and laughter, a threat of a negative label. Then you analyse the females who said they would not date a man who visited escorts and you again discover that it is stigma that governs their thought process.

They do not want to date a man that pays for sex because they cannot bear the thought of been seen with such a man. They know, society will gossip about them if they do. But men basically make a similar threat to women: "if you don't look attractive, then we will not like you." Thus, swathes of women must focus on beauty, essentially to again avoid the nefarious stigma. I remember a woman that committed suicide because her boyfriend at the time was caught with child pornography. Now this woman did not commit any crime. She had nothing to do with her boyfriend's evil deeds. Yet she committed suicide, simply because of gossip. She could not bear the fact that society would now laugh at her. They would point their fingers at her. She would always be known as the woman that dated the sex offender. What I am trying to assert is that humiliation and the threat of humiliation dictates society.

Despite all the crime no one thinks to ban interaction altogether to prevent crime. If you don't interact with society, you cannot be a criminal.

Live as if you are dirt famous and everyone can see everything you do.

Society is very adaptable. It can function through both harmony and conflict, and perhaps a mixture of the two at the same time. Harmony in this case would be traditional Native American society's. Conflict is modern day capitalism.

Take immature impressionable people and force them together, either through school, the office, the suburb where they live etc. That is all it takes to sustain society. The system is self-sustaining; a sort of sociological perpetual motion. Society maintains society. Society gives birth to even more society.

Ostracization, as in being the ostracized individual, makes us feel bad because it is bad for society. It is society trying to protect itself.

Being positively labelled makes us feel good internally and that is why we are addicted to it.

Society is in a state of perpetual psychological blind conflict in order to maintain its equilibrium.

To understand society you must understand the threat of stigma.

The foundation of being a good person is understanding stigma. It is the knowledge that if one behaves in a certain manner, one will be ostracized.

The unconscious fear is shielded by the essentiality of conformity. The unconscious fear is the Labelling Anxiety which masquerades as conformity.

The Labelling Anxiety is like dark matter. We cannot perceive it but it dictates our behaviour.

The reality is that you are a "good person" because you are deeply afraid. This Labelling Anxiety component of your psyche is in relentless operation. When you chat to the barista in the coffee shop, it is at work. "Do this and do that; don't do this and don't do that."

People are a mirror into our souls. What they think of us as they look at us determines how we feel. Give a man a mask, as they say. Erving Goffman was dead right. We are always actors trying to be approved and labelled correctly.

If you do not have an identity, you cannot be attacked; if you don't exist, you cannot be psychologically raped.

We all react differently to the psychological assault of being observed, just as there is variation in the result or outcome of a physical assault. If you were punched in the head, you may get a black eye or lose a tooth or break your nose or fall and hit your head off the ground etc. Likewise, when society psychologically assaults society, the response varies within individuals.

The threat of stigma functions just like stigma. Through the threat of stigma, you are as stigmatized as the escort or the schizophrenic or the rapist. This threat of stigma forces you to live the life you currently live.

The threat of stigma regulates us much more than actual stigma. If we defy this threat of stigma, we become stigmatized. The stigmatized individual then becomes a fallen angel, despised and ostracized from society.

We strive to avoid stigma and this in turn maintains the equilibrium within society.

Every interaction is a theatre of war. Imagine two people sitting opposite each other in a coffee shop having a chat. They both strive to be positively labelled by the other which means they both must positively label each other. Every act and word spoken is designed to maintain the equilibrium of the conversation.

The result of the sociological conditioning is a bit like looking at a house from both the inside and outside. You do not see when you look at that house, the foundation, the blocks, the wires in the walls, the plumbing under the floors and so on. Likewise, when you look at someone who is a married parent, working a decent job, living in a nice house and driving a nice car, you don't see the sociological pressures that led to such a person.

What you cannot see, is that when you expose yourself to other people, you become afraid of what they think of you.

"When you look in the mirror what do you see? Do you see the real you, or what you have been conditioned to believe is you?" - David Icke

The Bandwagon Effect: That everyone else is doing it, so must you to avoid being laughed at.

The genius is lauded, the serial killer vilified, but both once known are controlled by the prying eyes of society.

Analyse the celebrity. They love the adoration and approval. But it can all turn sour in hours. As in they can be cancelled. This dilemma also applies to the average not famous individual. They too demand approval from those in their immediate life. From their neighbours, friends, co-workers. And like the celebrity, they too can be shunned.

To paraphrase Kierkegaard; do it and you are stigmatized; don't do it and you are also stigmatized. It is impossible to make everyone within your life validate you.

The highest form of punishment within society is not being jailed or even tortured. It is being shunned.

What we call a decent person, is someone who wants to do good by society. They want society to approve of them. They almost feel a sense of guilt in not adhering to society's demands.

If there actually was a god, who played the judge, heaven would be empty.

Either we are not liked, which destroys us, or else we are liked but taken advantage of, which consumes us.

We struggle against the world, against society, and most people lose that battle. We would rather be accepted than be who we are. Ultimately, we are society's choices.

I remember reading about a man who was on disability for his bad hearing. He said that his mother, although not narcissistic, was putting him under pressure to get a job and have friends. Now analyse why she was doing this. She was doing it because she wanted her son to fall under the correct labels. In other words, she was afraid of how he was interpreted. She associated those who did not work and who had no friends, as being eccentric delinquents. When people asked her what her son was doing, she was embarrassed by having to tell these people that he was doing nothing. Again, she was governed by labels and she was not even a full-blown narcissist.

That we are narcissistic, we conflate or mistake happiness for approval. When people positively label us, we call that success. At least 50 to 60 percent of what we call happiness is based on sociological approval from those in our immediate lives.

Society regulates itself, but it is the state, the 1%, the ruling class, that truly benefit.

Unless you understand the sociological pressures that influence you, you are going to live a predictable existence and call it: "Living life to the fullest."

An unfortunate fact, but society is only as good as society is. If society is inherently narcissistic, then more of society will be narcissistic. If society is grateful, then that will lead to more people being grateful.

Fleeting pleasure is not worth a lifetime of regret. I suspect women understand this much better than men.

Understanding society is a very powerful advantage to have over anyone.

The reaction to stigma is the narcissistic pursuit of happiness.

"Stigma is a process whereby the reaction of others spoils normal identity." - Erving Goffman.

The ideal human is a social construct.

Social media spawn's narcissism within people. They unconsciously calculate that because they are distributing their identity publicly, they must conform in order to be approved. So, they become obsessed with self-image and hence narcissistic traits take over their conscience. "We are all just actors trying to control and manage our public image, we act based on how others might see us." - Erving Goffman. We behave in a way that enables us to be positively labelled.

How we conduct ourselves is a fabrication. It is illusory. It is all a response to being known. We are shaped by the economic system. The stereotypical man or woman is a fashion, a role that people play. "Most people are other people. Their thoughts are someone else's opinions, their lives a mimicry, their passions a quotation." - Oscar Wilde.

The Marxists wonder why capitalism has not been eradicated. Three huge components in why it prevails are A) You make the middle class fear each other. You expose them to the herd when young and they come to fear the interpretation of the said herd. This motivates them to conform. They are also very afraid to step out of line. B) You brainwash the middle class on Pretence Happiness. You tell them they can procure happiness by accumulating X, Y and Z. By getting married, having children, owning a house, a car, going on two holidays a year, buying the latest clothes and gadgets, that you can become happy. This is a material or narcissistic happiness. "If you don't do this, you will not experience life to the fullest," says the system. C) You give them just enough money to be able to afford this Pretence Happiness. Not too much, just enough.

It is a concentration camp without barbed wire. The middle class think they are living life to the fullest by conforming. All they are doing is contributing to the wealth of the bourgeoisie. That is their main purpose. But they hold the power (the middle class). They can if they were not so impressionable, rebel and demand a bigger slice of the cake. But again, it comes back to how happy they determine themselves to be. They are prepared to settle for such a small chunk of the profits because we brainwash them to.

The enemies of the middle class are the middle class themselves because through the threat of labelling, they enforce conformity. The person who deviates gets negatively labelled. This threat and the threat of not living life to the fullest makes them conform.

The enemy is not the Bourgeoise for they only reap the benefits of macro scale conformity. The enemy is the middle class themselves, that regulate each other through labelling. It is only when the middle class are not content, that they seek change. Deprive them enough and they rebel. You keep society obedient by keeping them happy.

Is it the carrot or the stick, with regards to the middle class? It is both. You make them afraid through labelling, that being the odd one out means they will be demeaned. That is the stick. The carrot is you implant in their minds the illusion of living the dream life, where they are above all else happy. Then you just give them enough money to procure this dream life.

The middle class through education, urbanization and parenthood, regulates itself.

The 1% only fear one thing: the middle class turning on themselves. If the middle class ceased having children, then the 1% and the politicians would listen, and very rapidly at that. The capitalists can decide how much of their wealth to share with you; but they cannot determine how many children you have, if you have any.

We do not know. That much is obvious. But to exacerbate the problem, we don't know that we don't know. We possess zero insight into how the economic system takes advantage of us. We are also lacking in realizing that we do not realize.

Animals only fear each other physically, not psychologically. Another cat is not afraid of being laughed at or demeaned by another cat. With humans, we fear other humans both physically and psychologically. If only one was cognizant of the viciousness of society, perhaps then they would retreat to a mountain and live off the land.

They say fame is fickle. The reality is that it is interpretation that is fickle. You just cannot depend on people to positively endorse you.

There are two states: One, the world of people you know and who know you. Two, the world of people you do not know and who do not know you. Anonymity is as vital as friendship for a healthy mind. When you are too known, it can cause problems.

Fame and criminality are the two extremes of being known. Both are unhealthy.

It is amazing how offensive just keeping to yourself is to some people.

You sacrifice seven tenths of who you are just to be accepted by the world.

In the Soviet Union, if you did not adhere to the communist idealism, you were sent to the Gulag. In modern democratic society, if you deviate from the group's interests, you get shunned. Being shunned is essentially its own Gulag. "When the people are being beaten with a stick, they are not much happier if it is called the People's Stick." - Mikhail Bakunin. This quote is terrific by Bakunin. When the stick is the government, people are miserable. But when the stick is other people, they are also miserable. Are people in democratic countries happier than those in China? Yes perhaps, but not by much.

It is simple really. Where you have society, you will always have oppression, regardless of whether it is the state or society itself that is the oppressor. The beauty of democracy is that people are blind to this oppression. They think they are free.

One essentially spends most of their life trying to accrue friends so that there will be a good turnout at their funeral.

These Right Wing commentators are to young insecure men, what the plastic surgeon is to young insecure women. Again, it is all about being liked and when you offer up a chance to become idolized, insecure people will swallow whatever poison you give them.

When the problem is being known, what then is the cure? The cure is to build a time machine and go back in time and try to reason with your young naive self, that the path you will take will only cause heartbreak.

Karl Marx wished that the workers of the world would unite and remove their shackles. But the workers of this world, as in the middle class, are in a war with each other that they cannot unite. They are so busy trying to outcompete each other in general as to who is the happiest, that the bourgeoisie inevitably gain. The average Joe is not jealous of the 1%; he is jealous of his co-worker John who has a better life than him. The bourgeoisie, through parenthood, education and other factors like urbanization, teach the middle class "how to be happy", and then give them just enough money to procure this happiness. It is through the pursuit of happiness (and the avoidance of stigma) that the capitalist regime is kept intact.

"When we give our minds and our responsibility away, we give our lives away. If enough of us do it, we give the world away and that is precisely what we have been doing throughout known human history. This is why the few have always controlled the masses. The only difference today is that the few are now manipulating the entire planet because of the globalisation of business, banking and communications. The foundation of that control has always been the same : keep the people in ignorance, fear and at war with themselves. Divide, rule and conquer while keeping the most important knowledge to yourself." - David Icke

The only difference between the right and the left with regards to stigma, is that the left is cognizant that they are stigmatized. With the right, everything they do in life is because that is the way you live. The left is more open to questioning what most take for granted.

I read something once, something that gave me great solace, and that was, that being happy in this world means disappointing people.

Being known is a perversion.

"What could I do in life that would lead to me committing suicide?" Very few people in life have the maturity to ask such a question, let alone answer it.

The economic system will destroy us if it has not already.

The price of existence as a human is being known. David Foster Wallace gave a great example of what motivates people to commit suicide. He used the analogy of a skyscraper in flames and the only option is to choose a less tortuous method of death by leaping from the said skyscraper. With regards suicide of people who are clinically depressed I would wager a large reason for many suicides (but not all) was being labelled. They did something and were labelled negatively, and this pushes them over the edge. The torture of being labelled is much greater than the pain of suicide.

There is so much anxiety associated with being labelled and man is the only animal that is afflicted by this threat. Through exposure we slowly strangle each other.
We need to label to police the system. To make it functional.

While we understand stigma, we also understand approval. In order to counter the almost insidious nature of being humiliated by society, we seek to earn society's adoration. But approval is just a stigma. You see this with adolescents that were bullied when in school. What is their response then? It is to seek approval through being successful, wealthy, beautiful, famous and so on.

Being looked at by another person is the same as looking into the mirror. And looking into the mirror is the same as being looked at by another person. Often the mirror is our greatest foe.

If you think of the famous person, they must live a very precision engineered life. Why? They do so because their identity is exposed to the world, who then threaten them with labels, should they choose to deviate from this precision engineered life.

"Choose your self-presentations carefully, for what starts out as a mask, may become your face." – Erving Goffman.

Camus once mentioned that the only way to deal with an unfree world is through an act of rebellion. Unfortunately, there is only so much behaviour that is tolerated within the current system. The individual can only rebel so much before they are negatively labelled by society.

Because of labelling, society is finely tuned. You can do A, B and C; you cannot do X, Y and Z.

What precedes conformity/capitalistic insecurity is the Labelling Anxiety; what precedes the Labelling Anxiety is being known; what precedes being known is existence as a human being.

Sartre said we are condemned to choose but we are also condemned to be labelled, despite doing nothing and our choices are severely influenced by the fact that we will be labelled.

Our problems are unquestionably interpersonal problems based on approval. Either we want to be approved or we want to maintain the fact that we are approved. For example, if you go for a job interview, to get the job you have to be approved by the employer. Then to keep the job once you have it, you have to maintain the approval from the employer. The same with a relationship or friendship. It can also be applied to other things such as why we are material in nature, again because we want people to see what we own or possess. We want them to approve of us. Thus, we live chaotic, if not miserable lives, just to impress people we don't really care about.

It is possible to be the kindest, most generous, most morally conscious law abiding person and still be ostracized in some way or form. That essentially is the conundrum we face daily.

Freud said we were driven by sex. Adler said it was over power. Frankl said we chased finding meaning. I would not disagree with them. But I also think we are driven to avoid humiliation.

Your Labelling Anxiety says: I need a partner; overcoming your Labelling Anxiety says: I can be happy alone. Your Labelling Anxiety says: I need a good job; overcoming your Labelling Anxiety says: I can work in any job. Your Labelling Anxiety says: I need to be good looking; overcoming your Labelling Anxiety says: I am not dependent on appearance to be happy. The Labelling Anxiety makes you insecure and makes you desperate. As a result of the Labelling Anxiety the two most common words in your unconscious mind are: I need. I need a partner; I need a good job; I need to look good; I need to be popular etc. And because you keep saying I need, you approach each day in uncertain terms. Essentially you become an agent of gratification wherein when what you need or wish for materializes, you feel good or gratified. But this gratification erodes into the night sky and you wake up anxious the next morning because you again need to hit targets in order to become happy (gratified). When you tackle your unconscious Labelling Anxiety you can rewire your brain to convey gratitude.

Evolutionary psychologists assert that the male and female differ regarding procreation. The male has multiple partners; the female carefully selects her partner. I do not disagree with that. But with humans one must also factor in labelling. The human male can have multiple partners and is labelled positively as a result. The female in contrast due to the threat of negative labels must be careful with how she has sex. The man who is promiscuous, metaphorically speaking, gets a medal; the woman that is promiscuous gets shamed. Now I do not agree with this shaming, but that is what happens and this is a huge component of why the female of society is obsessed with love, because it is the only system in which she can have sex and be positively labelled.

The "whore stigma" that we apply to the female with regards sex, is really a stigma against the male. The male reproductive organs carry such shame, that man is in ways a shameful animal.

The ontologically secure individual cannot perceive the effects of labelling.

To paraphrase my hero Durkheim, even in a world of saints, such as heaven, some saints don't get along with each other. Some saints dislike each other. The moral being, that on Earth, you cannot make everyone like you. That is societal nature.

The only way heaven works is if there is only one person in heaven. If heaven replicates earth, where you have billions of people living together, then heaven is going to have a similar suicide rate as that of real-life earth.

There is Collective Ostracization and Individual Ostracization. Collective Ostracization is being a convicted sex offender. Individual Ostracization is when one person does not like you. For example, if you get invited to a party or wedding and choose not to attend, then the person that invited you won't like you. They will negatively label you. This is Individual Ostracization.

Seeking a positive label is connected to the avoidance of a negative label. We want to do the correct thing only because we don't wish to be guilty of doing the incorrect thing, given the context or situation. To avoid stigma, we gravitate towards positive labels. The reality is that you are a model upstanding citizen married with two kids because you are purposely attempting to avoid a negative label.

People have a habit of blaming the powerful institutions such as the government, the army, the prison system, the psychiatric institutions and so on. But one must also blame society itself. Society is one of those powerful entities. The average man with short hair, dressed a certain way, living in a certain house, driving a certain car, behaving a certain way, is not motivated by appeasing the government or the army or the doctors; he is motivated in pleasing his peers. It is his partner, parents, his friends, his co-workers and so on, that decide him.

If you take the flight or fight with regards the Labelling Anxiety. You can either flee the anxiety through not being known or you fight it through conforming.

Man is the only animal that can be a genius or a criminal.

Fame kills; fame does kill. Fame is just a variation of criminality, albeit not as interesting.

Good honest people are incredibly anxious at being perceived as bad dishonest people. There are criminals serving life sentences in prison that worry much less than the standard free person.

One of the earliest signs of maturity in life is the realization of just how delicate life is. How it can all fall apart in the blink of an eye; how your choices can break you. "Hell is the truth seen too late." - Thomas Hobbes.

If the final step is a nervous breakdown, the first step is having devoted fans who would kill for you. If I could only give one piece of advice to anyone, it would be: Don't become famous.

The criminal fears being caught and the law-abiding individual fears being a criminal. The criminal is ostracized; the law-abiding individual fears being ostracized.

I guess the reason my most people are dumb is because the more intelligent and mature you become, the more worried you become.

We live in an age where it is all about individual gain, and quite ironically that is what enables society to flourish.

Our relationships are really agreements. Person A says hello to Person B and Person B reacts by also saying hello. If you violate the agreement, you get shunned. The price you pay for being known by someone is you can be shunned at any time.

There exists a bind. The economic system promotes interaction, but we then become subservient to the interpretation of those we interact with.

Are we patrons of conformity or victims?

In the concentration camp we commonly call life, interpretation is the barbed wire.

Our actions determine our labels. Even if you do nothing, you still get labelled.

The tragedy for western society is that they are so sure they have not been manipulated and this is one of the triumphs of capitalism.

Social media is bringing Franz Kafka's The Trial to life. Being known is violence because you become a slave to one's interpretation of you. What social media does is magnify this violence.

The most damning indictment of the current system is that even though we do not freeze or starve, we are still anxious. Forget about our genius to predict the atom or our artistic merit, society still currently is drenched with anxiety. We talk about eradicating disease and preventing climate change and they are necessary things to do. But one other thing we must do is eliminate anxiety as well.

Success is not without its demons.

It is kind of a sociological paradox (The Stigma Paradox!). If you could turn off stigma in society, that will at the same time lead to a decrease and increase in crime. If there is no stigma, then there is no crime, which leads people to doing more criminal acts, that are not criminalized, because of the lack of stigma. Which does not make sense. Crime cannot rise and decrease at the same time. This would lead me to believe that stigma must always exist in society. The curious question is: Will you always have stigma because you have crime or will you always have crime because you have stigma? Which comes first or do they interchange? I think on reflection they occur simultaneously together. You will always have both. One doesn't come before the other. They both occur at the same time.

That you have labelling, you have stigma (and the threat of stigma). That you have them two things, you have crime. All occur simultaneously.

The Stigma Paradox proves that you will always have crime in society because stigma can never be turned off. If hypothetically you could turn off stigma within society, you would reach a sociological singularity where society breaks down and nothing makes sense. Thus stigma must always exist and because it must always exist, crime must always exist in tandem. Where one is the other is occurring simultaneously.

If you turned off gravity in physics, the universe would not exist. Similarly with stigma (and the threat of stigma) in society. Society just does not exist if you turn it off.

The conformist and the schizophrenic are both troubled by the same anxiety (Labelling Anxiety). But their retrospective unconscious minds respond to it differently.

Franz Kafka's The Trial is indicative of the power of being known. Imagine you are a conventional individual minding your own business and keeping within the law, that is suddenly arrested for an unknown crime and paraded before the public. Your identity will go from being resolute in not being known to being terrified of this new label which is the result of being known. You will despair at how society now perceives you. This is why I remark, that to be known in this world is to commit existential suicide because once known you are labelled and once labelled you are controlled. Opinion makes life unbearable.

While the right is applying stigma, they are also very conscious of the fact that they could be stigmatized themselves, and hence act and live to avoid it at all costs.

To be known and to be labelled are the two sides of the same coin. You cannot be known if you are not labelled and you cannot be labelled if you are not known. If you are not labelled it means you are not known and likewise if you are not known, you cannot be labelled. The consequence of being known is that you are labelled and if you are labelled it is understood that you have become known.

We are in effect psychologically violating people through labelling them. Just by being in the presence of people, by being seen by them, is psychological violence upon your identity.

The pressure to conform, through the labelling phenomenon and labelling anxiety, which is enforced by socialization, is blind and unconscious in its operation. One is not aware nor cognizant that their response to exposure to society is to best manage their presentation. So long as we interact with each other, the Labelling Anxiety (the avoidance of stigma) is abundant and never ceases.

This avoidance of stigma is a huge part of the equation of why we are who we are and why we do what we do.

"Man is nothing else but what he makes of himself," famously asserted Jean Paul Sartre. Unfortunately, man is severely restricted or limited by society in what he can make of himself.

Facebook would have us believe that we are all friends with each other, which is far from the truth. Really we are trying to out compete, or at least match, those who we count as our "facebook friends."

There is not a man that has ever lived that has not been shunned in some way or form. When I say "man," I mean men and women alike.

If we were living in George Orwell's 1984, where every single thought, let alone mistake, was publicly known, there would be no society, as we would all be in the Gulag.

We live in a world of continuous threats. People are bombarding the individual with threats through labelling them.

We regulate society not just through money but also through interpretation.

Success changes you and often not for the better. Fame is a terrible price to pay for anything.

We are condemned to exist, then condemned to choose, then condemned to be known, then condemned to be labelled and finally then condemned to despair.

Dying is not the worst thing in life; being known is.

Presentation Management dominates modern society and perhaps dominated older societies as well. The reason we say hello to people we know is presentation management. We want them to positively label us, as they do us. The reason we are law abiding morally good people is again Presentation Management. In this case we desire the whole of society to label us positively.

To counter humiliation within society, we chase success. Success makes us look good which in turn makes us feel good with respect to society.

A fatal error so many make is that they think success guarantees happiness. Not necessarily. One must see the destructive side of success, that you can pay a terrible price for it. As Truman Capote said: More tears are shed over answered prayers than unanswered ones.

Think back to when you were an adolescent. You were consumed by image. You needed the correct clothes, the correct haircut, the correct everything etc. You needed these things because you wanted to fit in with the crowd. You did not want them to laugh at you. Your mind became programmed on desire to be happy and hence you became an agent of gratification. You then simply carry this mentality into adulthood where you need the correct life. Maturity is eroding this diseased mentality.

We can only label because we can use language. Labelling is a product of language.

Paradox of exposure: We need company and yet we fear it also.

Ending stigma, whilst good for the individual, is not necessarily good for society. If you ended the stigma against sex offenders, the rate of sex offences would go up. Similarly, if you ended the stigma against those that are HIV positive, the rate of infections would climb. Again, if you end the stigma against women with regards sex, less women will get married, which would be detrimental for society. For every person that must live with stigma, as horrible as it is, you have another person desperately trying to avoid a similar fate. Stigma is really society's safety fuse. The purpose of stigma is in part to enable society to sustain itself.

Stigma is a disciplinarian tactic used by the capitalistic right to keep society in check.

What is the textbook schizoid individual trying to do by being anonymous? They are trying to avoid the consequence of being threatened with stigma. They know without understanding it fully, that when you immerse yourself within society as a loner, you get negatively labelled.

Racism, sexism, homophobia, mental illness stigma etc. is subtle nowadays. It still exists, but it is covert. If you are overt about it, you get in trouble. For example, a thirty-year-old woman is immediately prejudiced when she walks into an office for an interview for a new job. The interviewers, despite never suggesting it, think to themselves that she will be off work for two years soon with a pregnancy and hence do not hire her. If you have a serious mental illness like bipolar or schizophrenia, you will not be hired for most professional roles. The stigma and prejudice still exists, but it is covert and subtle.

I do not think certain commentators (I will not name them) fully understand stigma with regards to the professional environment and the role it plays in determining whether someone is employed or not. A woman through virtue of her sex, a black man through virtue of his skin colour and a schizophrenic through virtue of their mental illness, are all negatively labelled. This negative labelling then contributes to the final decision-making process of whether they are hired or not.

If you think of the Labelling Anxiety with respect to some infamous criminal such as Pablo Escobar, who was a Colombian cartel boss. In order for him to accumulate his wealth and power he must expose himself to people. These people include rival bosses, people of authority such as army personnel, lieutenants who might want to take his position and so on. These people make his life troublesome. That he has exposed himself to these people, he comes to fear them. What is the reverse? The reverse is that he retreats to solitude on some mountain and lives off the land. But he has no wealth in such a position. Now you must apply this to the average law-abiding citizen. In order to make money and own a house, they must expose their identity to people, and they come to fear the interpretation of these said people. They can choose to negate this anxiety by living on welfare but will possess a poor standard of living.

Man is the only insecure animal in existence.

To remark that everyone is a threat is not paranoid. It is existential.

Interaction is the source of all our woes. No interaction equals no crime.

The female's obsession with beauty is a direct response to being known by men. Likewise, the male's obsession with money or success is a direct response to being known by women.

You simply cannot have society without stigma. This stigma leads to people wanting to out-compete each other, which greatly aids society. No one wants to turn up at a wedding all alone. The same can be applied to socializing or going to work. We are aware that presenting a good image is vital to not be gossiped about and gossip is just a form of stigma. So, the next time you feel uncomfortable or even nauseous about being gossiped about or perhaps having to take part in gossiping about someone else, console yourself that this gossip is vital for the functionality of society.

Anonymity is one of life's little-known pleasures.

Once we label someone, we remember them.

The minimalists should apply their philosophy to people and not just possessions.

The wild animals may worry about food or predators, but they never worry about being liked.

If fame is horrible, then so is being known, because fame is just the extreme end of being known.

We take existence for granted when we feel melancholic because we are not liked.

One can only be happy in solitude. But are you prepared to defy the herd that imposes people on you? "A man can be himself only so long as he is alone; and if he does not love solitude, he will not love freedom; for it is only when he is alone that he is really free." - Arthur Schopenhauer.

I said in previous notes: "Trust is the source of our woe." I was wrong because before trust comes interaction. You must interact with someone to trust them. Therefore, interaction is the source of all our woe. Interaction makes us insecure.

Which gender does gossip affect more? Or is it equal? I suspect, excluding those who are full blown narcissists, that the female of society is more affected. First, less females commit crime. Secondly, vastly more women than men have poor body image. Thirdly, the cosmetic industry is dominated with female clients. Fourthly, women when it comes to a relationship are greater influenced by what people will say of their partner than men. Fifthly, more men are comfortable with living in solitude than women.

We either wish to avoid the dreaded stigma or maintain the fact that we are liked. Both are identical in their functionality.

Being sociologically mature is not the same as being existentially mature. Maturity is being both. Most people are sociologically mature. They understand how to behave within society. Unfortunately, very few are existentially mature. How many see the universe as they live day to day? Very few I would guess.

Franz Kafka understood the bureaucratic nature of social interactions. With Metamorphizes, the character wakes up as a Cockroach. In a sense we are all Cockroaches in society or at least we try desperately not to be perceived as one. That is the threat society carries as you interact within society. Then with The Trial we see the result of losing one's reputation within society. Reputation is another thing that people strive to maintain. How do we maintain our reputation? How do we prevent society from treating us as a Cockroach? We do so by earning societies illusory approval and to earn it we need to be a married parent. It's called living the dream life, but it is in actuality managing one's presentation to such an extent that they will be accepted by society.

The female element of the herd are ruthless and merciless. Any woman who decides to deviate from the path of marriage and family is labelled fittingly. This fear haunts the conscience of the young naïve woman. Faced with the threat of being an individual and being labelled a heretic, she conforms implicitly to appease the tribe.

You have never been alone and that is why you are lost. You go to school, then college, then work. Predictably, only when you retire at sixty years of age do you understand how you were deceived.

There is a pattern immerging with reality television stars, in that a good number of them commit suicide after exposure. They do so because they have become labelled.

The man who goes alone is often seen as the alpha male; the woman who goes alone is treated as a leper.

We are condemning ourselves through psychological rape masquerading as friendship.

People will wonder what I mean by saying we fear being known. Narcissism by default is the fear of being known, the fear of being labelled. That is why narcissists are extremely status conscious. But think of the individual who has plastic surgery or spends an hour in the gym or obsesses over buying the latest clothes or gadgets, they do all those things to be approved, by other people, but also by themselves. In other words, they fear being laughed at and hence fear being known.

We are all Instagram models without the fame. We depend on partners, friends, co-workers to approve of us. We have been so inured from a young age with regards meeting people and socialization that we don't sense the threats. We cannot detect the fear that accompanies being known. We respond to it unconsciously though.

That society does not adapt to us and never will, we then are forced to adapt to society. When you have lived your whole life in a sociological cage, you don't know what true freedom is. And even if you possessed the key to liberate yourself, such is your acclimation, you probably would refuse to use it. "It is difficult to free fools from the chains they revere." – Voltaire

With animals there is no psychological threat. A kangaroo is not afraid of being laughed at or demeaned by another kangaroo. Humans are afraid of being laughed at and demeaned by other humans.

There is such a problem with sexual crime and yet they will not ban sexual interaction outright. They won't do that because they (the powers that be) recognise that in this concentration camp we call life, people need to have sex, to start families and give birth to the next generation who will contribute to the economic system. It may sound extreme but if you ban interaction completely, in other words make no one be within ten yards of each other, you will remove a lot of crime from present day life.

It is interaction that makes sinners and victims out of all of us.

If you take someone who works in a professional environment, male or female, they have a certain dress code they must adhere to. Ask yourself, why don't they come into work dressed in shorts and a t-shirt? They do not because they know they will be negatively labelled by co-workers and their boss. The threat of being negatively labelled has influenced their behaviour.

Labelling is a means of social control.

You can't erase your identity from the minds of people that know you. Once they know you and you them, your fate is decided. This is how the herd promotes conformity. Imagine you went viral tomorrow. Apply that same degree of apprehension to your life as you know it now.

The individual conceives that when people positively label them, they will become happy. But this is why they do not become happy because not everyone positively labels them. In the end they get slaughtered by their own craving for likeability. The trick is to overcome this narcissism and limit being known. Take for instance a social media blogger. That they are exposing their identity to the herd, they conceive that they need to look well. But after a while the audience gets bored or even negatively labels them, so the individual in question tries to become more beautiful in order to receive applause. They might have plastic surgery or spend a fortune on new clothes or starve themselves for a new body shape. But this mechanism is not enjoyment or happiness; it is suffering; it is being at the mercy of the interpretation of whomever labels you.

The Hedgehog's Dilemma can be applied to labelling. When you interact with people, you risk being labelled negatively by them. You avoid them completely and you suffer because you are human, all too human.

That we have parents and are educated we learn not to see people as threats. Instead we are taught to have friends, to get to know people, to socialize. But these things only increase our angst because we become subordinate to the opinions of others, of the tribe.

Shame is a masterful influencer.

Gossip is to the present world what the Gulag was to the Soviet Union. It is a means of inciting fear within the public to obtain their obedience.

The world with stigma is bad; but a world without stigma would be much worse.

One must understand that society and the individual are not the same. What is good for the individual is not necessarily good for society and vice-versa.

Gossip is a form of regulation. It precedes actual stigma.

A battle rages in the heart of the narcissist. They want to be talked about but not gossiped about. It is a conflict. Thus, their immediate response is to seek adoration. But adoration and the hunt for it is just another form of regulation. It functions just like gossip.

The one thing we all crave when we are young is to be liked. To fit in and to be approved. To not feel unnecessary. From this stems the pursuit of happiness and the avoidance of stigma.

When I use my fists, it is a physical assault; when i use my eyes, it is a psychological assault. When you punch someone in the face, they get a bruise; when you look at someone in the face, they adjust how they present themselves. We are always adapting our presentation in response to society observing us. But to reiterate, this adaptation is the response to a psychological assault through both eyesight and language combined (The Labelling phenomenon.)

You cannot be positively labelled without being negatively labelled. We ideally want to only be positively talked about and to avoid the nefarious gossip. This is not feasible in society. The price of chasing a good label off some section of society is that a different part of society will in turn negatively label you. At best the only thing you can do is try to not be labelled at all, whether it is positive or negative. But most in society either cannot forgo the allure of the positive label or else they are forced to expose themselves through work and friendship to society, in which case the positive and negative labelling dilemma is applied. What I am trying to infer is that if you socialize and expose yourself to society, even with the best intentions, people will invariably negatively label you. I repeat you cannot seek positive labels without exposing yourself to the risk of negative labels. You cannot have one without the other. So, this whole narcissistic dream whereby everyone in society will love you once you are rich or famous or beautiful will not materialize.

Those who despise you in ways save you. They teach you how to behave in society.

If the divorce rate is so high in some countries, why bother getting married? Again, return to the two threats: happiness and stigma. Marriage is hyped up as the only way you can have a happy life and if you don't get married you will be miserable. Secondly, the threat of stigma: god forbid what the neighbours will say of you if you don't get married and have two kids.

"We make our own hell out of the people around us." - Jean Paul Sartre.

Success leads to more people knowing you, and that by its very nature can lead to unhappiness as much as happiness.

As counter intuitive as it sounds, unhappiness is beneficial to society in ways. Unhappiness gives birth to the pursuit of happiness through the family unit.

Intelligent aliens from another planet would say our society is ill. But it is precisely this sickness that enables it to flourish.

If narcissism were bad for society (not the individual) then society would suffer, as in it would cease to exist. That society continues to persevere must only mean that narcissism is a component in its sustainability.

Anything that goes against society must be stigmatized, marginalized and if possible criminalized.

Which is the preferred option, if you were forced to choose: To be universally despised or to seek approval from everyone you meet? It is the former. It is better to be disliked than to live in fear of being disliked.

The stigmatization of the individual leads to the threat of stigma to everyone else, which contributes to society. The rapist for example is a subtle threat to other men: "Do what he does and you will be labelled "a rapist" yourself." Thus, other men dont rape. What this in turn suggests is that stigma plays a vital role in the sustainability of society, because as I say, where stigma is, the threat of stigma is. For example, we gossip about (stigmatize) those that may be law abiding but don't get married. This stigmatization is a subtle threat to everyone else: "If you don't get married, we will gossip about you also." Thus this threat influences people to get married, which contributes to society.

Stigma is not just the sex offender. The stigma we apply to the sex offender is the most extreme form of stigma and justified at that. But stigma at its most basic is gossip and it is the most common form of stigma. It is also the stigma we seek most to avoid (because it is so widespread.) Gossip permeates modern day society much like space-time does the universe.

Not one single human alive is 100% good. They just appear good. They deceive us. Or more to the point, we deceive each other.

If we were to apply the same laws we apply to the famous, to everyone, the whole world would be cancelled. Society has regressed under cancel culture. And society only grows when it forgives, not ruins.

Either you choose you, or society will for you.

People are not cognizant of the violence of speech and eyesight combined.

True maturity is realizing what choices will lead to suicide before you have made them.

We are blackmailed by our incessant need to be validated. We worry over who approves or does not approve of us. But ultimately what matters is that you approve of you.

Cancel culture is democracy's equivalent of a gulag.

There is a conspiracy at play, a great terrific conspiracy. And it is called society.

If you were married to someone who stressed you out, the logical thing to do is break up with the person. Likewise, if you were eating something that caused you some sort of pain or malady, you would stop eating that certain something.

Thus, if society is making you miserable, the logical thing to do is distance yourself from this said society.

We need to be able to label for society to function. Take this for a thought experiment: imagine if we had no identity. As in we had no name, no achievements or criminal record, and we all wore the same mask. Basically, we could not distinguish between each other, as in we are all essentially the same. In such a society, that we cannot positively and negatively label each other, means there is no incentive to out compete each other. As such that society does not function. Whereas in modern day society, we can positively and negatively label each other. We aspire to be like the people we positively label; we feel a sense of fulfilment when we compare ourselves and our life against those who we negatively label. This competition to outdo each other only exists because we can distinguish each other. As in it only exists because we can label each other. Thus, inequality is vital for healthy society's, as is insecurity and narcissism. Part of the reason communism failed in the Soviet Union is because everyone was ironically classified as equal. Thus, everyone was treated as the same. There was no positive and negative labelling. Thus, there was no motivation or incentive to be entrepreneurial. Capitalistic societies and economies thrive on the fact that we want to be better than everyone else. Keeping up with the Jones's is vital for a functional society.

Who is more affected by the threat of being gossiped about? I suspect women and that is part of why most crime is committed by men. Then, who is more affected by being gossiped about? I think it could be equal enough between the genders.

"Men are rarely aware of the real reasons which motivate their actions."- Edward Bernays.

A consequence or fallout from gossiping about others is you become afraid of being gossiped about yourself.

Friendship, much like a relationship, means we must behave in such a way to maintain the friendship. We must behave in such a way to not be ostracized by those who are "friends" with us.

We are effectively socialized against our will when young and then we become forever known by our peers and forever condemned by them. Imagine for instance you get invited to a wedding by a close friend and you do not go. Now the friend thinks that is rude and falls out with you over it. You then are attacked by guilt and remorse. Now imagine you had never known this person. There would be no guilt over them. What this says is that the people we know control our behaviour. They determine how we feel about ourselves.

A large portion of our lives is spent trying to make people like us or maintain the fact that they like us.

Our actions determine our labels and the threat of being labelled determines our actions. You live, but also die, on the choices you make.

You cannot fall out with friends if you have no friends.

Conformity and labels are linked. In conforming you become labelled; being potentially labelled endeavours to implore you to conform. So, if conformity is linked to labelling and labelling is linked to schizophrenia, then conformity is linked to schizophrenia. I believe the brainwashing to conform when young has a bearing on the disease.

"Our existence precedes our essence," said Sartre and in vying for purpose we adopt conformity and in doing so become labelled. Our essence precedes being labelled.

In our hunt for purpose we invite demons. We make ourselves but in making ourselves we label ourselves.

Existence ———— Essence ———— Labelled

Fig 5: *Bear in mind that once man exists, he is condemned to be labelled. He cannot not be labelled. Even if he does nothing, he becomes labelled (A loner; eccentric; strange etc.)*

The price of existence is choice and the price of choice is being labelled. Even the man who does nothing does something.

Fame is the most repugnant form of being approved.

We try to give up gambling or smoking or drinking but never interaction. Interaction is seen as something we must do. Interaction is the source of so many problems with the individual. If you can learn to live without it, you can be so much more assured in your existence.

We care deeply about the opinions of people whose welfare we do not actually care much about. A contradiction of sorts. As we walk up the street where we live, we are afraid of being gossiped about by the neighbours. Yet if one of those neighbours died, the world would not end.

Gossip is a vital cog in how societies sustain themselves.

Normative Social Influence is a type of social influence leading to conformity. It is defined in social psychology as "the influence of other people that leads us to conform in order to be liked and accepted by them." In other words, we try to be positively labelled by other people and we achieve this by conforming.

Given today's world, if you made everyone famous overnight, we would all be executed by the firing squad at dawn.

The Right/Left political divide owes itself in part to the threat of stigma (The Labelling Anxiety). The Right's response to the threat of humiliation is to earn approval, chiefly through living the material life. The Left's response to this labelling anxiety is to question the very system, which includes questioning the motivations of the Right themselves. Both owe themselves to society and by society I mean parenthood, education and urbanization. For example, a woman who was badly bullied for being unattractive in school takes one of two paths: A, she has plastic surgery to make her more physically attractive. This is the response of the Right. B, the response of the Left, she starts to attack the system. As in she starts to blame the whole culture whereby women must be physically attractive to be approved.

During World War Two in the UK, the suicide rate dropped, the admissions to psychiatric institutions dropped and the schizophrenic rate dropped. Then once the war ended, they shot up again. What one can deduct from this is that modern capitalistic society makes us miserable.

That we are seldom alone in life, through the educational system and work, we learn how to live within society. What we are blind to is how this living within society shapes us.

You are taught how to live within society and as such you can teach yourself to live in solitude also.

You would think that the riches of capitalism would make us happier, when in fact they make us unhappier. Why is this? One of the reasons, as Durkheim may remark, is that we put severe pressure on ourselves in response to the threat of being labelled. What I mean by this is that we see what other people have and A) either try to mimic them or B) try to outcompete them. We are exposed to people and we instinctively think that if I just obtain X, Y and Z, then I will impress these people and hence will feel good about myself. The person is perpetually saying "I need." "I need to date that person," which means "I need to be seen with that person." "I need to buy that car or dress," which means "I need to be seen driving that car or be seen wearing that dress." It is hard to explain, but the greater the quality of life, it seems the more desperate people become to accrue adoration. Approbation becomes the currency of happiness. But when you rewind back all the dominos, one of the first dominos to fall is socialization. We expose children to each other, and they then come to fear each other. You then teach them that being a grateful loner is wrong and you will be laughed at if you do that. The fear of being laughed at, otherwise known as being negatively labelled, has a huge influence in how they behave.

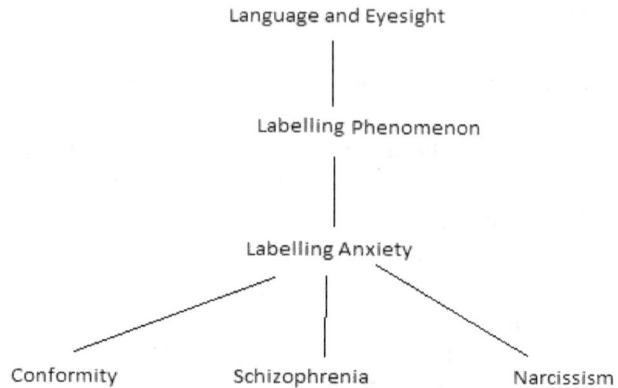

Fig 6: *Language and Eyesight give birth to the Labelling Phenomenon. This in turn gives birth to the Labelling Anxiety. Three (and there are more I suspect) responses to the Labelling Anxiety are Conformity, Schizophrenia and Narcissism.*

Labelling and Schizophrenia

What if schizophrenia was just a different response to life in the same way that one conforms is a response to life itself. Being known is stress upon our unconscious mind. Being known is a psychological assault on our minds. With schizophrenia, this process is faulty. Their response to this psychological assault is madness.

The root of schizophrenia is laughter (labelling). You have to remember that being known by another human being is a psychological assault upon our conscience. Conformity is just a response to that assault, as is narcissism and what I theorize, so is schizophrenia.

Think of it like this, you are not afraid of being laughed at by a Kangaroo; you are afraid of being laughed at by your parents, your friends, your co-workers and society overall. As I said earlier, think back to the dawn of mankind and one human being laughing at another human being, tormenting him with this ridicule. This laughter is a form of violence upon our conscience.

What I am trying to suggest is that there is a sociological aspect to schizophrenia. It is really caused by the violence that society carries by threatening to humiliate you through being known.

Schizophrenia is not a response to eyesight on its own and nor is it a response to language on its own. It is a response to the combination of language and eyesight that produce the two-dimensional Labelling Phenomenon. Likewise, with narcissism.

You can better understand the cause of schizophrenia if you treat it as a response and not just a disease of the mind.

Schizophrenia is caused by the Labelling Anxiety and hence malfunction to the Labelling Phenomenon. The hallucinations and delusions are malfunctions in the Labelling Phenomenon. The way they perceive the two-dimensional field of eyesight and language (the combination that is the Labelling Phenomenon) is gone awry.

Take for example The Labelling Phenomenon in a healthy person as they walk down the street. They avoid bumping or interacting with people they do not know. They say hello and perhaps chat to those they do know. They always behave in a certain way to maintain a positive label. Nothing out of the ordinary. Now take the malfunctioning Labelling Phenomenon in someone who has the positive symptoms of schizophrenia. They walk by a person they do not know and think that "he is out to get them." Or they see two strangers talking together and think they are "talking about them." Their Labelling Phenomenon, how they perceive the reality of this world, is defective.

Imagine if you were walking through Alaska all alone and suddenly you encounter a grizzly bear. Straight away you would go into flight or fight mode. Now apply the same reasoning to walking up a busy shopping centre all by yourself. Instead of the threat being physical, it is now psychological. And how are you psychologically threatened by all these people you are ignoring as you walk by? By laughter, which is a neater term for the Labelling Anxiety (the threat of stigma.)

I cannot emphasize it and I apologize for being redundant. The Labelling Anxiety causes the defective Labelling Phenomenon in someone who has schizophrenia. How society interprets them and how they register this interpretation (how they are labelled and how they react to this labelling) leads to the malfunctioning Labelling Phenomenon.

Schizophrenia is not a madness; it is simply the Labelling Phenomenon reacting in a different way to the bombardment of labels by society. To test the theory, I would argue four things: One, someone who cannot speak a language, will not develop schizophrenia. Two, if one was stranded from birth on an island away from society, they would not develop schizophrenia. Three, if we could only see in a different wavelength of light, schizophrenia would not develop. Four, if we were blind from birth schizophrenia would not develop. I theorize that if you are born blind, you cannot develop schizophrenia. You cannot because you cannot see the faces of people and hence cannot be attacked with their interpretation of you. You cannot be labelled by them.

Madness and normality are frames of reference. Neither one is more correct than the other, only more convenient.

Is schizophrenia an adverse response to life or is life an adverse response to schizophrenia? If schizophrenia were an illness of the majority, it would not be an illness. Maybe it is normal life that is insane.

With schizophrenia the individual's own pressure to conform to society's principles is in battle with the fear of being labelled (engulfed.) The narcissist fails to conform; the schizophrenic refuses to conform.

If you want to get inside the mind of schizophrenia read RD Laing's The Divided Self. The real difference in the mind of the schizophrenic lies before the storm. The end is madness, but the means is existential. Now in my philosophy there is no healthy individual psychological-wise. Those who conform are as clinically insane as those in the psychiatric hospitals, but what psychiatry deems a healthy individual is one that wants to expose their identity to the world, chiefly to the people in that world. With the schizophrenic, this exposure is detrimental to their unconscious mind.

RD Laing was approaching this in his book, The Divided Self. What does it mean to be known as a human in this world? When you understand that proposition, you can understand the steps that lead to schizophrenia. I am not really breaking any ground. Rather I am just re-wording what RD Laing said. My interpretation of his theory is that schizophrenia is a disease of being known.

What anthropologists should study is whether there is a link between schizophrenia and humiliation. In my theory of it, I speculate that around the time we learned of humiliation (through language), schizophrenia first started appearing in ancient civilizations.

Schizoid PD (which is a precursor to schizophrenia) is not really a Personality Disorder. It is more of a different way of perceiving the reality we come to know as the economic system. Such an individual has a different mentality to the world as we know it. Their ethos is dysfunctional to the current economic system.

The interesting thing about schizoids is that they find security in anonymity. This is counter intuitive to life as we know it. What psychiatry deems a healthy individual wants to have friends, a partner and a job. They want to expose their identity to the herd. To the schizoid individual these things only make one insecure; they make one behave a certain way; they provoke anxiety. The schizoid thus finds refuge in being unknown. As shocking as it sounds, one can learn a lot from them. In other words, one can try to limit being known to be more secure and hence happy.

How your mind unconsciously reacts to being labelled is the difference between conformity, suicide and schizophrenia. As Laing detailed in his great book The Divided Self, the schizoid individual who becomes schizophrenic, eventually in order to protect his identity, stops being identified. This is the defining moment before the storm that is the psychosis. When he seeks to protect himself through being unknown (not being labelled) his mind implodes much like a supermassive star. Therefore, I remark that schizophrenia is a disease of labelling because such an individual (Schizoid) strives to defend his existence through not being labelled. But this in turn precipitates the madness of schizophrenia. (Please read chapters 7, 8 and 9 of RD Laing's The Divided Self)

If you took someone who was psychotic and someone who was deemed normal and introduced them to intelligent life from another galaxy, that intelligent life would not be able to deduce who was normal and who was ill.

Sartre's "the look" is in my opinion the root cause of schizophrenia.

How two humans know each other differs radically from how two dogs know each other. Humans fear a negative interpretation. They fear a negative label. They are afraid of being laughed at. Animals cannot idolize or shame another animal, but humans can do so to another human. The method by which humans label one another differs from how animals label each other. The mechanism by which we know each other (other humans) is different. It is a form of assault.

If you were attacked on the street randomly, you would remember the attack and quite possibly the face of the person who attacked you (should you see his or her face). Likewise, when you immerse yourself in society you remember people. For example, if you start a new job, you will remember the identity of those new co-workers. Or you remember the identity of school friends and so on. The point I am trying to make is that if knowing people causes you to remember them, much like you would remember someone who assaulted you, then the simple act of being known is violence upon your identity. For example (and I have used this repetitively throughout these notes) as you walk on a busy street and pass by people you don't know, your mind just ignores them. It cannot even remember them (their faces). But if you meet someone you do know, you are required to greet them and they you. If you walk by them without acknowledging them, they will feel insulted. Thus, their interpretation of you is a form of violence upon your mind. The fact that they know you forces you to behave a certain way. How they interpret you determines how you feel about yourself. Their recognition of you is a psychological assault.

Schizophrenia is a disease of sociology and not just individual psychology.

What if the people you remember in a positive way (parents, friends, co-workers) were processed as being deviant or violent?

There is similarity between being physically assaulted and being psychologically known. Both are forms of violence on our conscience. Both can cause psychological malfunction.

RD Laing once said that schizophrenia was a sane response to an insane world. It is an interesting way of looking at it. Is schizophrenia an illness or is it the normal world that is ill? The schizophrenic is not out of touch with reality; reality is out of touch with the schizophrenic. In other words, is love and work, things we take for granted, the true illness in human culture. In some ways I agree with Laing. I have tried to point out with these notes (particularly through labelling) how other people impinge on your psychological security. But the ordinary "sane" individual cannot see this for they have been since youth socialized against their will. Vandalizing one's identity through meeting people becomes second nature to such an individual. Love and work are instilled in the minds of the sane; they cannot tolerate any other system. Consequently, through such a conformist methodology they become more insecure. They become slaves to image, money, friendship and sex all because they are initially a slave to interpretation. Much like drinking seawater their minds become existentially thirstier as they expose themselves to more and more people. On that premise, the schizophrenic or schizoid individual that Laing characterized in his great book The Divided Self, actually goes out of his or her way to protect themselves. They get labelled dysfunctional by society, but they are more secure than the standard conformist.

If it turns out that labelling is a component of schizophrenia (and I could be completely wrong) then it is first and foremost a disease of language because without language humans cannot label the way they do.

If we all had to wear the same mask, like some Muslim women wear a burka, then life would be so much easier. Schizophrenia would decrease, as would narcissism. If we all had the same name, the same face and the same personality, schizophrenia would not develop. If we could not distinguish each other, schizophrenia would vanish.

Labelling and Society

We are used to thinking that everything we are accustomed to is part and parcel of life and living life to the fullest. This is not entirely true. So many things are derivatives of the economic system. And if the said system were to fracture or disintegrate, so too would the many things we presently appreciate in life.

Modern society tries to make you as anxious, depressed, miserable, insecure and as desperate as possible, because it knows full well that your reaction will be to try to become as happy as possible. And as I suggest in all my non-fiction notes, this response is predictable.

To paraphrase the great adage, there is no fate, only what society makes of us.

"It is society which, fashioning us in its image, fills us with religious, political and moral beliefs that control our actions."
- Émile Durkheim

The average individual possesses extremely poor insight into how insecure and otherwise malleable they are.

It is society that must be content in life and not the individual.

We are not nothing, but we are not much either, because we are ultimately what society makes of us.

What kind of people does the economic system need to sustain itself? One, it needs people who know nothing other than the ability to consume. Secondly, it needs people who desire to be happy, if not happier than those in their immediate life. And thirdly, it needs people who are absolutely petrified of being laughed at, should they not conform.

One should never doubt the power of: "What would the neighbours think?" in shaping who you are.

You will not earn universal adoration anywhere in life. Your neighbourhood, where you work, through fame etc.

One must understand that this labelling anxiety, this threat of stigma, is everywhere. It haunts the individual second by second. So much of who we are in life is a reaction to this threat of stigma. It is a violent arena we inhabit. Our response to this very violence determines the things we buy, the things we do.

We are threatened with being labelled rude, so we acknowledge people we know when we see them. We are threatened with being labelled lazy, so we must work. We are threatened with being labelled odd, so we get married and have two children. Daily life is plagued with these threats of stigma (negative labels.)

In a world of continuous threats, we thus become devoted servants of presentation management. We want to fit in. We do not want to be gossiped or demeaned. That is a huge reason why we want to live the dream life. Look at what we do to the person who does not get married: "He is mentally ill; she is a lesbian."

I agree wholeheartedly with Mikhail Bakunin. Where you have people or society, you will always have the state and hence oppression. Even if you just had two people, one would take on the role of the oppressed, and the other the oppressor.

The healthy society is where The Right and The Left have a voice. The unhealthy society is where only one of them has a voice. A healthy society is one where the person you hate has a voice. In fact he is probably a multi-millionaire. The opposite to such a society where everyone has a voice, is Cambodia under Pol Pot.

The system is shrewd. It turns the middle class against each other and through that it obtains their consent and acquiescence.

When the ordinary Joe's of this world conflict with each other, they lose sight of how the rich take advantage of them. Capitalism fosters a competitive nature within its minions and through this it attains their devoted loyalty to the cause of making the wealthy wealthier.

Most people do at some point, perhaps only for a brief moment, question the system. They recognize that they are being taken advantage of. All I am trying to do is enlighten them as to how that happens.

We are the children of the economic system.

"We laugh at sheep because sheep just follow the one in front. We humans have out-sheeped the sheep, because at least the sheep need a sheep-dog to keep them in line. Humans keep each other in line. And they do it by ridiculing or condemning anyone who commits the crime, and that's what it's become, of being different." - David Icke

We are not humans with free will in this capitalistic environment. We are actually the choices and decisions we make, which more often than not are determined by the society we inhabit.

Society always seeks to protect its own interests. Society is one single entity. It is not a collection of free individuals, behaving as they so wish. On the contrary, it is like a gazelle whose sole purpose is to survive the tense and terse landscape. And the threats are never ending.

It is most difficult to be mature in life; but it is impossible to be mature within society.

Women are vastly more sociological when it comes to choosing a partner, which means the threat of stigma plays a bigger role in how they choose a partner.

If your anxieties are societal, then so too are the methods you use to alleviate this said anxiety.

Slut-shaming is to women what being a pervert is to a man. It is a disciplinarian technique designed to regulate women so that they will become a married parent.

The proof of stigma is society, because if there was no stigma, then society would collapse.

Ending stigma would be like an influenza pandemic, except a hundred times worse. The whole framework of society would deteriorate.

As the economic system adjusts, so too does man. But when man seeks to change, that change is resisted by the economic system. Man can only be what the system directs him to be.

It takes low IQ, stupidity, unintelligence and ignorance for society to flourish. Because those that are dumb all calibrate happiness in the same way. One, they have to have the family unit; two, they have to buy more and more things; three, they have to have enough money to fulfil points one and two.

In times of crisis, such as a viral pandemic, the person you live beside or work with, becomes a companion. There is a sense of solidarity and social cohesion between you and them. But in times of normality, that same person is treated like a competitor that you must better in every aspect of your existence.

Richard Dawkins famously remarked that you cannot reason with those whose faith in god is fanatical. It is utterly pointless. No matter what you suggest, they will not listen. Similarly, with someone who is obsessed with the dream life at forty years of age, you cannot reason with them.

"It is not the consciousness of men that determines their being, but, on the contrary, their social being that determines their consciousness." - Karl Marx

Things we think are bad for society, such as narcissism, stigma, insecurity, crime, unintelligence, actually may be beneficial for society. The logic is this: If they are so bad for society, why does society continue to flourish? The reason is because they are bad for the individual, but good for society. Unhappiness is a good example. If unhappiness within the individual is considered bad for society, why does society continue to function? The reason is because unhappiness actually benefits society in ways. Those who are unhappy exclaim that they will become happy once someone loves them or they live the dream life, both of which contribute to society.

As children we adhere to society. Then in our teens and twenties, we go through a period of rebellion. Then when we settle down in our thirties, we become socially conscious as if we were children again, and remain so until our death. But it takes the despair and confusion associated with our teenage years, to grow into a mature person in your later life.

We despise people that ignore/shun us as much as those who harass us. The criminal of society is not just that man who commits a crime.

I quoted Irvin Yalom in previous notes, in how he remarked that a woman once told him that it was only when she had a terminal illness, did she learn how to live. Similarly, it is only in times of economic crisis, does society learn how to live. In times of peril, the goal is to survive, which galvanizes the soul of society. But in times of economic prosperity, the goal is to be happy, which ironically enough is why so many are profoundly unhappy.

We live placid lives of despair and this is passed off or marketed by the system as living the dream life. There is so much that we do that we wish we did not; there is tragically so much we want to do, which we cannot.

Intelligence is very dangerous to society and that is why most people are dumb. It takes intelligence to understand society, but idiocy to run it.

Society is the reason you want to be rich; society is the reason you want to be beautiful; society is the reason you want to work the dream job; society is the reason you want a million followers on social media; society is the reason you want to be married with two children. The only way you cannot absolutely covet those things is to unequivocally avoid society altogether. Society is the price you pay for being known and it is an inequitable exchange. To exist we must pawn our very existence.

There are primitive tribes in the Amazon basin that are culturally more mature than hedge fund bankers earning millions on Wall Street.

The game is rigged. You have no freedom. You have been conditioned to believe you have. Everything that is legit and considered right, is only because it benefits the economic system in some way. Analyse how in America or the Uk or Spain or Italy and other countries how the governments of those supposedly free states were able to lockdown the areas during the Covid 19 pandemic. What you have to deduce from this is that everything you are accustomed to perceiving as part of being free and living life to the fullest, actually benefits the state, the ruling class, the wealthy and 1% in some way or form. Democracy is an illusion, but the best illusion available. "The supreme law of the State is self-preservation at any cost. And since all States, ever since they came to exist upon the earth, have been condemned to perpetual struggle — a struggle against their own populations, whom they oppress and ruin, a struggle against all foreign States, every one of which can be strong only if the others are weak — and since the States cannot hold their own in this struggle unless they constantly keep on augmenting their power against their own subjects as well as against the neighborhood States — it follows that the supreme law of the State is the augmentation of its power to the detriment of internal liberty and external justice." - Mikhail Bakunin

Look at Covid 19 in democratic countries, which are supposedly by the people, for the people. The governments of those democratic countries were able to lock down the whole society. That is the kind of power that Stalin or Mao had. Another example of the power of the state is the femicide rate in democratic countries, which is largely just ignored. It is ignored because those in power know how important marriage is to the economy.

Mental illness is as much a sociological problem as it is a psychological problem, because if you removed society from the equation, a lot of mental illness would vanish.

To be part of the group or any group, is to be an utter ignorant fool.

Just by keeping to yourself and avoiding people altogether, is a sociological crime in itself. It leads to being shunned.

George Orwell was spot on with his prediction of the future. The only thing he got wrong was who is doing it. Not the state but society.

I once thought ideas could change the world. I was wrong. God could write a book about what is wrong with you and it still would achieve nothing. As long as parenthood, education and urbanization remain, you will have a society the way it currently is.

It is a conflict-driven society we live in, not an altruistic-driven society.

What is deemed good in life, as in the way to live, is determined by the state because it benefits them in some way, shape or form. That the state benefits, means they do not criminalize it, which means they do not stigmatize it. Society then reacts to this.

I see commentators mention that the ethos of the far left that is sweeping western civilization is draconian or authoritarian or extreme. But one must remember that men and women of previous centuries were too faced with such an extreme ethos, albeit different in method, that made them conform. The result of the far-left ethos of present is a more inclusive society for the LGBT community. The result of the ethos that has dominated society since the dawn of modern civilization has been the pressure to marry and have children. It is ironic then that the far-right attempts to resist the change that currently sweeps society in the west, when for literally millennia, society has been in ways oppressed and the result of this oppression is society.

Modern society does not forget, and certainly does not forgive.

How ironic, the Buddhist monks in Tibet are vastly happier than their narcissistic counterparts on Wall Street, despite not possessing nearly as much as the banker or hedge-fund manager. Modern society does not allow one to be grateful. Uncertainty is the enemy of gratitude. When you must pay bills and feed children, whilst working in a job that could vanish next week, it is exceedingly difficult to be grateful. So, people automatically substitute this for gratification. If they get a job promotion, they feel gratified; if they buy something new, they feel gratified. And so on.

Yes, society goes a long way towards making you diseased. But the fools continue to blame society and then do nothing. Society will not make you better. It is not in its nature to do so. Society is the virus and only you are the cure.

"A modern soldier returning from combat---or a survivor of Sarajevo---goes from the kind of close-knit group that humans evolved for, back into a society where most people work outside the home, children are educated by strangers, families are isolated from wider communities, and personal gain almost completely eclipses collective good. Even if he or she is part of a family, that is not the same as belonging to a group that shares resources and experiences almost everything collectively. Whatever the technological advances of modern society---and they're nearly miraculous---the individualized lifestyles that those technologies spawn seem to be deeply brutalizing to the human spirit." – Sebastian Junger

The same people who make you feel good by complimenting you, are the same people who can torment you by insulting you. If you live for external validation, you thereby expose yourself to potential slander. The trick really is to seek validation from within. Be your own god and your own executioner.

"None are more hopelessly enslaved than those who falsely believe they are free." - Johann Wolfgang Von Goethe.

The state, through the instrument of society, owns and controls you. The state, again through society, decides your purpose and meaning in life. Purpose and meaning that ultimately benefit the state itself.

People cannot wrap their heads around the fact that a healthy society contains crime. A healthy society contains a stable crime rate. Societies that have too much crime are unhealthy and that is understood. But societies that have no crime, are also unhealthy, such as Nazi Germany or Soviet Russia. For example, if you started sending everyone that commits a crime or everyone who you think will commit a crime, off to a concentration camp, that will only lead to society becoming still born. People in such a world will be too afraid to leave their houses. They won't interact with anyone else. The marriage rate and hence the birth rate will decrease. And as such, society will suffer. It will disintegrate. In the quest to create the perfect society, you create an imperfect society. If you make the consequence of committing a crime so grave, that people won't commit that crime, they also wont get married and have children, out of the fear of doing something criminal. The other point, which Durkheim touched on and I agree with, is you need the bad to have the good. You have to stigmatize a certain percentage of the population (label them criminals) to enable the remaining percentage to behave in the correct manner.

Nothing beats deviance for bringing society together. Deviance galvanizes the herd. It leads to social cohesion.

Labelling and Morality

"Fear is the mother of morality." - Friedrich Nietzsche.

We are the only animal that has laws. Why do we have laws? We do so because we are able to interpret and we can interpret because we can speak. Thus, if we could not speak, we would not have these laws and would rely on pure animal instinct. Furthermore, we will always have crime because we can interpret what we see. Crime is just a negative interpretation and interpretation is life.

There is no judiciary amongst the Hyenas of the Serengeti. Morality in part stems from the threat of being labelled. It is not that we are inherently good; it is that we fear a negative interpretation (label).

Man is the only animal that can sin. Why do we have these laws? So, the system of economies will flourish. Then people assume that because such and such a person broke the law that he is bad or evil. There is no right or wrong; good or bad; just our interpretation of what is right or wrong.

Crime will always exist because crime is a derivative of interpretation and interpretation is a derivative of language.

We are all criminals waiting to be born.

We are all potential criminals; that much is certain.

Laws are not constants of nature. They are something we have given birth to.

We are moral only because we fear being labelled negatively by society. This then channels us into behaving a certain way.

Thus, all these laws are just things we have concocted as humans to placate economies.

We either choose a system of anarchy or a system of economics.

The difference between the man that does and the man that does not is choice.

There is no disparity between us; the misdemeanours of one man are the misdemeanours of all men.

There is no right and wrong in life. We adopt a model for what is right and wrong and use it as the standard. We do not argue over what is right, but over what is convenient.

If you live long enough, you eventually become a criminal.

The jails are full not with people who committed crimes (there is no crime in this savage universe) but with people who are dysfunctional to the economic system. We use the labels of crime to incarcerate them like lepers all because they do not contribute in a good way to the economic system.

We all have the potential to be amoral. All it takes is choice.

"There is nothing either good or bad but thinking makes it so." - William Shakespeare.

The same atoms that constitute your body are the same atoms that constitute a tree. That we have consciousness enables us to fool ourselves into believing that we are special, that we have meaning, that we go to heaven.

Wouldn't life be so much easier if we all just avoided each other. Criminalize sex, sport and socializing. Criminalize any interaction between humans. This way they will not commit any crimes. Ok, human civilization will be extinct in a hundred years, but there would be a stark reduction in crime. I am not trying to be facetious, but the point I am trying to make is that crime is a direct result or a by-product of the world we live in and a world without crime can only exist without a world as we know it.

Nihilism: There are no rules despite the judiciary. Everything is in this universe permitted. We are just a species of animal raging against nature.

Kill someone in your country and its murder. Kill someone in the name of your country and its patriotism.

All the laws and all the opinions are designed to control society and society is a beast that cannot be tamed. This perfect utopian world where everyone's opinion is validated or achieved does not exist. This concept of heaven on earth where everyone never experiences a negative reaction to a preceding action is an illusion. Events in life don't always materialize as one thinks they should. You have good days and bad days. You win the lotto and your house gets robbed. Bad luck is here to stay as long as man is.

An accident investigator once said that there are so many car crashes in part because cars drive so close to each other, thus increasing the risk of a crash or interaction. One just must accept it as part of driving that one may be in an accident if they drive, even if it is not their fault. One cannot just decide not to drive their car. How would they get to work? How would they get to the shopping centre? What if everyone then decided not to drive any longer to not be involved in a crash? Economies would break down or falter. The same can be applied to human interaction. It is because we interact with each other that negative things happen. Likewise, the solution of everyone just avoiding everyone would ground economies to zero. Accidents or more to the point crime is a product of human interaction. It is a by-product of life as we know it.

Two things constitute a crime: The action and the interpretation of that action.

There is a terrific quote by Jung: "No tree can grow to heaven unless its roots reach down to hell." From a sociological perspective this is most certainly true. The moral law-abiding members of society are only good because they know they can be deviant should they behave a certain way. Nobody is born good; they learn as they grow up what is considered wrong and seek to avoid it, and that is what makes them appear good.

There is no crime without interpretation.

Interpretation: What makes something right or wrong? Is it right or wrong with regards the universe or because we interpret it to be right or wrong?

A good gauge of a society or culture lays in how they treat animals.

Dog fighting is one of the failures of humanity. Mankind is shameful but nature is often no better.

Life I think would be much simpler if we did not exist.

Paper money is fiat money, in that we apply worth to it. Similarly, the rules in functioning economies are "fiat rules," designed to enable the system to sustain itself.

The deviance of supposed saints sells much quicker than the continuous crimes of the sinners.

I dreamed of a world where we had no journalists, lawyers or psychologists.

The criminal is condemned; so too is the ordinary citizen. He is condemned to be moral.

We fear being alive as much as dying.

Society sees freedom; I see fear.

Do atoms go to heaven? Somehow, I do not think they do.

The human body is composed of about 55% oxygen atoms. Now contemplate this: Do the oxygen atoms in the air that you breathe in as you read these notes have worth? Do they have value or meaning? Do they go to heaven or fall in love? No, they do not. So why then should humans, when all we are is 55% oxygen atoms.

You should not do to an animal what you would be put in jail for if you did to a human.

At heart we are all murderers, but the moralistic of society make a conscious decision not to kill.

I cannot help but think that violence is our innate nature and that the civilized modern society we have come to cherish is a consequence of our conscious reason.

There is no law without language.

Truth be told we are all perpetrators; we are all victims.

Tragedy bleeds change.

"Freedom is nothing but a chance to be better." - Albert Camus.

Interaction must be thought of as a drug like alcohol or gambling. When you interact with people you increase the chances of doing something negative. If they criminalized interaction you would create a safer society. Crime is a product of a society that interacts; sexual crime is the product of a sexual society that interacts. Criminalize interaction and you will see a stark reduction in any crime.

The world you see around you is sculpted by being known. It is being moulded by labelling.

The laws are designed to prevent people going to jail and not to actually put people in jail.
Life on earth is illusory. Where else in the universe will you find love and work?

It just demonstrates how normalized we are on the current system, in that despite all its failure and violence, we never think to ban interaction to create a safer society.

All the problems in life stem from the fact that we are free. Free to do what we want; free to act and hence free to err. If you just curb this freedom you could prevent so much crime. And yet the citizens of this world would never contemplate such a world. They want to be free to do what they want; they want to be free to fail.

Such is the economic system that someone or something suffers along the way.

Everything you see around you is not because of god, not because of intelligence, not because we are human; it is because of language. The universe is language.

We are free to kill and that we choose not to is what makes us human.

Arguments: The biggest waste of human endeavour, not because they lack entertainment but because they lack a winner. "A casual stroll through a lunatic asylum shows faith proves nothing," said Nietzsche. Your conviction, your argument, your interpretation is about as correct as that of an insect.

Reminisce over the hyenas eating their prey alive and such brutality may just provoke you into being grateful for mankind's dominance. The animal must contend with prey, with starvation, with dehydration, with hypothermia, with disease, with parasites, with mankind etc. What are the capitalist man's worries? That he is not desired or liked. How many animals are being slaughtered right now as we speak, to fuel man's hunger or vanity? We really and truly have it so good and we take it all for granted.

We control society with the law, but we also control them with their dreams. We tell them how to live the dream life.

It is all an illusion: Work, love, wars, religions, sports teams, violence, beauty, money etc. It is all an illusion relative to the universe. With respect to the universe life is but an atom in the Pacific Ocean.

Someday it will be man versus man in the pit. Our abuse of animals will turn on us.

Why is one system righter than the other? It is our thinking that makes a system right or wrong and not that they are fundamentally right or wrong.

We say machines, but who designs and manufactures the machines. It will be economics that will destroy us. We need money, we need jobs, but in order to create them we need a new product. Eventually we will give birth to something that will turn on us and the singularity will be long passed.

The reality is there are no rules; everything is permitted. But people become so radicalized on being moral that they see the criminals as alien.

Ultimately the judiciary is in operation to placate the economic model.

If patriotism is our incest, then idolatry is our adultery.

One of the things that most disgusts me about human nature is how we shift the goalposts so to speak. We commit murder in the name of war and give medals for it. We slaughter animals in their millions to fuel our hunger and we justify it.

We shift the goalposts to pander our inherent bias.

Intelligent life from another planet would have a great laugh at all the contradictions human beings create to enable the economic system to thrive. Murder someone on the street and you get put in jail; murder someone in the name of war and you get a medal. Beat an animal in public and again you get put in jail; murder them in an abattoir and you get a salary.

Society isn't moral because they are inherently moral. They are moral because they fear being labelled amoral.

In the future married people will be criminals; in the future all crime will be committed in the bedroom.

Labelling and the Pursuit of Happiness

The pursuit of happiness is not just an ideal but a form of regulation.

What we commonly call "modern day happiness" is nothing more than a drug addiction. It causes more misery than heroin.

What you commonly call "living the dream life," is in actual fact a state-run enterprise that benefits the ruling class in some way. Everything that is legit is only so because it benefits the state in some way. "If there is a State, then there is domination, and in turn, there is slavery." - Mikhail Bakunin

"There are invisible rulers who control the destinies of millions. It is not generally realized to what extent the words and actions of our most influential public men are dictated by shrewd persons operating behind the scenes." - Edward Bernays.

The pursuit of the material life does not make you happy. At best it only makes you satisfied.

One becomes fulfilled at meeting the conditions society has imposed on them. But such satisfaction is not happiness nor gratitude. And it is fleeting.

Living the dream life more likely than not will only make you satisfied and not exactly happy. One cannot be genuinely happy with having to work within society. But they are satisfied. But there is a difference between satisfaction and happiness.

If happiness and misery are opposite ends of a scale, most people in modern society lean towards misery.

We live as if we are facing an egg-timer and it is not death that frightens us, but rather the prospect of being unhappy when we are forty years old.

In youth, we are all idealists, and it is in our very nature to misperceive satisfaction for happiness.

To better yourself you must first defeat yourself. It is who you are in life, and not where you are, that fundamentally makes you happy.

Narcissistic happiness is societal, unlike gratitude. Those who are narcissistic desire to be happy so others can see them as such. They are possessed by society. For example, the wedding day for the entitled female is basically an event for her to demonstrate how happy she is in life compared to others. Love, where you are in it to show off to everyone, is most certainly not love at all.

We work stressful jobs, just so we can earn enough money, just so we can buy things we don't need, just so we can post pictures of ourselves on social media, just so we can impress people who would not bat an eyelid if we were knocked down by a car and killed.

Because of biological and sociological pressures, it is not a question of what you will be in life, but more of a question of what you will not be.

If you grew up and lived all your life on a secluded island, hundreds of miles away from the nearest human, you would not have Starbucks nor McDonalds nor Mercedes nor Manchester United and so on. But the one thing you would have on this lonely island, is happiness. The avalanche of insecurity, self-pity and general unhappiness that pervades modern life is caused by society.

Modern happiness is most certainly societal in source. You could ask your neighbour what he or she wants to do in life in order to become happy, and they would give the same answer as you do. You could ask your work colleagues and again you would find a similar answer. In fact, you could ask most of society and 95% of them would say the exact same thing you said. You have been conditioned to measure happiness in a certain way, conditioning that you ultimately are blind to. "Most people are pawns on a chessboard, led by an unknown hand." - Dark (TV Series.)

Do you want to be happy through being satisfied or do you want to be happy through being grateful? That is the big choice you face when you become an adult.

Satisfaction is herd driven. What I mean by this is that one is satisfied only when they feel they impress society.

Satisfaction can deliver its own dose of happiness, but it is chaotic. Such happiness fluctuates. You receive a job promotion and you feel good. Your child gets in trouble at school and you get stressed out.

Satisfaction is driven by labels. It is because one wants to feel the sensation of being satisfied with the life they have, because they want to be seen by society living that certain life. They want to live "the dream life" because they want to be seen living it, and when they are seen with such a life, they thus feel a sense of satisfaction, almost narcissistically.

Satisfaction thus is vital for society to function, in contrast with just being happy through gratitude. Those that are grateful are not compelled to make others be impressed with them and henceforth are less likely to chase or even acquire "the dream life." For the grateful, they are just happy to be alive, which although is extremely beneficial for the individual, it is not so beneficial for society.

Very few people are happy because very few people can be grateful. One can only be grateful in solitude with stress and uncertainty minimized. What people actually are is satisfied through being gratified by the image or representation they portray to society. What they inevitably do is analyse who they are, where they are and what they have, and then compare this to society in general. If they exceed society in this respect, they declare themselves to be happy. But if they possess less or interpret themselves to be inferior, they then surmise that they are unhappy in life.

You can sort of empathize with the individual that is addicted to feeling satisfied. The gratification that one receives when people admire them has no match. It is like the high one gets from injecting heroin for the first time. But like heroin, once never suffices. Such a person needs to keep receiving external validation in order to become gratified, which only makes them suffer.

I recall watching an interview with a pornography actress and she was asked what motivated her to take up porn. She said she became addicted to men giving her compliments. The approval she got of men, had no equal, she remarked. Secondly, she said that she could not bear the thought of losing this validation or endorsement. One can apply this to the greater world. We become addicted to earning approval as the currency to be happy, and secondly, we cannot envisage a world without it once we are caught in its web.

The pursuit of happiness should actually be called the pursuit of satisfaction.

By wanting or wishing to become happy, you can at best only become satisfied.

The sense of inferiority, and the perception that others are happier than you, plays a crucial role in society because the means to alleviate these persistent feelings of inferiority is and always has been, to attain the dream life.

Two words that should never share the same sentence are "fame" and "happiness."

If you are engaged in comparing your life to others, you invite suffering. You do so because in order to be happy you must out-compete everyone else from a labelling perspective.

In today's age, looking happy takes precedence over being happy. People would rather be narcissistically satisfied than be grateful.

Everyone you encounter asks whether you are married or have children or where you live or what car you drive or what job you have. No one asks if you are just happy.

Modern society and gratitude are mutually exclusive. Modern society does not allow people to be grateful. There is just too much uncertainty associated with such an existence. What people are is narcissistically satisfied. When they succeed in some way, they experience a high that fills them to the brim, for a short while, until it evaporates and needs to be experienced again somehow.

With satisfaction, validation must come from external sources. With gratitude, validation comes from within.

It is far easier to be satisfied through being gratified than to be happy through being grateful. That is why so many gravitate towards this Fast-Food-Happiness.

Competition within the individual leads inevitably to regulation. So many within society are trying to do better than those in their immediate life. They call it living when it is how they are in part regulated. Their own mind works against them.

"We consume, as we produce, without any concrete relatedness to the objects with which we deal; We live in a world of things, and our only connection with them is that we know how to manipulate or to consume them." -Erich Fromm.

Labelling drives the pursuit of happiness because people want to be satisfied with how society labels them. In other words, they want to look happy, which is not happiness at all. But this looking happy manages to fulfil them in ways, so long as they keep looking happy in front of the observing herd. Which basically means they must keep earning money, or looking attractive, or succeeding, or having sex and so on. But in between the peaks of gratification there are troughs of shame and self-loathing. Such a person cannot bear these persistent feelings of failure and do instinctively what comes naturally to overcome them, which is to succeed narcissistically in some way again. And so, the cycle continues.

To be grateful one must overcome the persuasion that society afflicts upon the individual.

It is quite amusing in that people are both at the same time happy and miserable. A capitalist contradiction of sorts. They are miserable because they must work long hours for poor money with even poorer job security. Yet they attest that they are actually happy because they are satisfied that they have a job, a house, a car, the family unit.

We are alienated, as Karl Marx put it, especially in the present narcissistic culture we inhabit. We are living in a sociological bubble. We have no awareness of the universe and our place in it. Modern society has us alienated from ourselves.

David Icke made a great point once that if you want people to adopt a certain philosophy or idea, make it seem that it is their own idea. Now David Icke meant it in a different context to how I mean it. But the concept is true. What the economic system does most effectively is condition people to believe that their dream of being a happily married parent by forty, is their own idea or decision. No, it is sociological. This dream life that you want to live when you are forty years old, is the result of non-stop social conditioning that was implemented upon you since you were four years old.

We condition people to be of the belief that they are not conditioned. That is a fundamental component of any type of brainwashing, be it a religion or the economic system.

The right says: "The reason you are not happy is because you are not married with two children." The left says: "The reason you are not happy is because you are married with two children." Personally, I side with the latter.

Happiness is the easy part. It is having the correct attitude that leads to this said happiness that is the difficult part.

The world is a marketplace where happiness is the product, and as such people compete to see who is living the best life.

The future, despite its seductive nature, is never worth sacrificing the present for.

The first step on the path to maturity is to accept that you are ignorant.

The common denominator among insecure people is that they all want to be happy. And secondly, they all calibrate this happiness in terms of living a certain way.

The devil reveals himself through your desperation. Whatever that may entail.

The pursuit of happiness is actually the pursuit of satisfaction, which is driven by labels. One seeks satisfaction to counter the threat of stigma.

I would estimate that most people, sixty to seventy percent, think they know why they want to be a married parent, but actually are too dumb to understand the actual reason for their life choices. It is the Dunning Kruger Effect or a variation of it. You take a man who has wanted to get married since he was fourteen years old. He thinks he has decided this himself, devoid of influence. But he cannot see the evolutionary and sociological pressures that compel him to become a married parent by forty. He is greatly confident that he understands the reasons why he wants to live a certain way. When in actual fact he is dumb and overconfident about his abilities. Such a person is smart enough to do his job, but he is not existentially mature. He has no awareness of the universe just as he has no awareness of the conditioning implemented when young that funnels him into conforming.

Rollo May, Viktor Frankl and Erich Fromm both said in different ways that those that are happy in life are the very people who are not desperate to be happy in life. It's a sort of contradiction.

Contemporary man, as Karl Marx alluded to, is alienated from his fellow human beings. When we were hunter gatherers, there was a sense of social cohesion and solidarity within the group. Everyone worked in unison to maintain the survival of the group. In modern capitalistic societies, the person you work with or live beside is a competitor who you must out-compete in every aspect of your life. To add insult to injury, we are alienated from ourselves also.

We are not who we want to be. We are alienated from ourselves by modern society. We are puppets on strings, a sort of sociological mannequin, crafted by society itself.

To paraphrase Jiddu, the moment you want in life, you can never be happy, only satisfied.

When I suggest that one is alienated from themselves, what I am attempting to convey is that one is not who they truly wish to be, but rather they are what society tells them to be. Modern capitalistic society has poisoned the individual. The solution then proposed by this toxic system is to make everyone like you. Hence people become consumed by wealth, beauty, fame, success etc. "When people like me, then I will like myself; when people like me, then I will be happy." That is what such a conditioned person says.

The whole objective of the capitalist regime, from parenthood to education to work, is designed to alienate man from himself. He loses his individuality and becomes identical to everyone else, in his aspirations and his failings. In essence, he becomes robotic.

Erich Fromm remarked that in order to love, one must be able to live alone. It is the exact same with happiness. In order to be happy, one must, and I emphasize this, be able to live alone. I am not suggesting that one does, but rather that they can if needs be.

The pursuit of satisfaction is a huge part of the sustainability of the capitalistic system.

The dark truth is that the system can make people work all their life and to suffer stress in order to make other people insanely rich. To add insult to injury, they are willing to sacrifice their health for such ideals. If you conveyed that message to young adults in the schools and colleges, a lot of them, if they had any wits about them, would reject the system. But what we actually convey to these impressionable young adults is that you can be happy (it's a lie) when you are forty years old, if and only if you are a married parent. And because society effectively regulates itself and that we are so desperate to be happy, we adopt this philosophy as a truth. The sordid truth is that at best, such a person that attains this "dream life" only becomes satisfied and not actually happy.

If you want to change the system, if you want the wealthy to distribute their money to the poor of society, take to the streets and refuse to have children. Wealth is nothing without society. Let's say for example, that a virus pandemic wiped out 99% of the world's population. Then the billionaires, if they managed to survive, are no longer billionaires. In a world of anarchy, we would all be peasants; starved, frozen and without hope.

It is a contradiction. People desire to live life to the fullest, to be independent and free. But this living exposes them to society, which then curtails their ability to live and be free.

Evolutionary psychologists have long asserted that people thrive in small groups and not larger ones. It is the individual that has a few close friends and a partner, that is more than likely mature, in contrast to the individual that needs a million followers on Instagram.

People excel in life when they know less people and not more. But this is most difficult for the individual to attain. For starters they must be educated with other children and young adults. Secondly, they then must work for forty years with other people. For instance, it is well documented that Native American groups were far happier in how they lived than those in modern society. Reasons for this are because these Native American groups were small and thus there was a sense of social cohesion and social solidarity, which is evidently lacking in modern capitalistic and narcissistic societies. As urbanization increases, so too does the rate of depression, anxiety and misery. What does society do to us that makes us suffer? It is not society but the system that encompasses society, specifically what we call modern capitalism. You may still have the same society, but the rate of the three things I just mentioned decreases during times of war and anarchy. Again, why is this? As I have attempted to suggest in all my notes, being known (being labelled) in modern society wreaks havoc on our conscience.

"The mass of men lead lives of quiet desperation," famously asserted Thoreau. This is very true. There is so much we wish we could do, but we are restrained by society.

Is it not astonishing: crisis galvanizes the human spirit; peace destroys it.

So many men and women cannot sacrifice wealth and beauty for anything else because they are drug addicts. Their narcotic of choice is approbation.

The Eagles once sang that the things that please you, can often hurt you somehow. It is true. The life you are accustomed to, that yields snippets of satisfaction, can often be the source of long-term friction. What is the solution? At best you can only react differently to how society interprets you. You cannot prevent society from labelling you, but you can determine how you respond to how society labels you. Gratitude is the best response. You do not respond to such a provocation with your mouth, but rather with your mind. Change your attitude and you will conquer all.

Life must be a recurrent resurrection. Its goal should be the hunger to be better than you were yesterday or last month or last year. For the foolish of society, they try to out-do their peers and not themselves. "The whole life of the individual is nothing but the process of giving birth to himself; indeed, we should be fully born when we die - although it is the tragic fate of most individuals to die before they are born."- Erich Fromm

"A relatively primitive village in which there are still real feasts, common artistic shared expressions, and no literacy at all—is more advanced culturally and healthier mentally than our educated, newspaper-reading radio-listening culture." – Erich Fromm.

Labelling and Love

I must apologize for remarking (In Remarks On Existential Nihilism) that all sex is violence. I now regret suggesting that.

Love is the biggest response to stigma. We are taught by all the propaganda that love is the means to live the dream life. It is actually the means by which we carefully manage our presentation.

What the heterosexual relationship really amounts is the means to have sex, guilt free and stigma free. That is a huge part of its allure.

Men and women are biased towards marriage because the system itself is biased towards marriage. We are just doing what the system tells us to do.

Love is linked to stigma and hence labels. Love is a safety mechanism for people, especially the female. It protects them from stigma. For instance, imagine if love vanished right now. It just disappeared. Now when two people have sex, in this love-less world, it is because they are both using each other for their own sexual gratification. They become an object by which they both achieve an orgasm. They almost become alienated by each other. Secondly, in this loveless world, it quickly becomes apparent that the economic system is also using both. It is using them to provide children for the said economic system to sustain itself. Now return to our world of love. In this case the two people that have sex with each other are classified as partners or soulmates. Sex in this case is all part of a healthy relationship. "We are madly in love," such a person might remark. They use love to overcome the feeling of being a sexual object. They suppress the feeling of being alienated through romance. Then secondly, with regards to the economic system, again those in love that have two children, are doing it because they endeavour to live "the dream life" in love. In their minds, they are not been taken advantage of by the economic system, because marriage and children is all part of love, so they remark.

Because of society, a relationship becomes commoditized, just like a product in free market capitalism. In the free market, the intention is to have the superior product. When you apply this reasoning to the product that is the materialized relationship, the objective is to as to who looks the happiest.

It is the state that romanticizes love. They don't mention its violence, just as the lotto does not mention all the people that buy the ticket each week and win nothing.

(I must apologize for what I wrote in previous notes for zoning in on the female of society with regards social control and stigma. It also plays a huge role with the control of the male of society.) For example, men, through threatening to label women whores, regulate women; women, through threatening to label men perverts, regulate men. The amalgamation of these subtle threats is love.

What is the result of stigmatizing men who visit escorts, stigmatizing escorts themselves and in general the slut-shaming of the individual? The result is most people get married in order to achieve sexual fulfilment, which is extremely beneficial to society. Stigma is vital for society to prosper.

We call the women who are escorts, "whores." We call the men who visit them, "perverts." This leads to most men and women marrying to be sexually fulfilled.

The male that has numerous sexual partners is a creep or a pervert or a sex pest. The female that has numerous sexual partners is a slut or a whore. Most are cognizant of this and thus strive to avoid being labelled as such.

The reason love is advertised as romantic is because that is what it takes to seduce you into contributing to the 1%. The reason it is romantic is because it is not stigmatized, and the reason it is not stigmatized is because it is not criminalized, and the reason it is not criminalized is because the 1% is biased towards, and the reason they are biased towards it, is because they gain. The birth rate is what they (1%) care about because that is what sustains their wealth and power.

Women play an extremely important role in regulating society because they ostracize men who are deviant. The man who uses women for casual sex, the man who visits escorts, the man who leaves his wife for another woman, are all shunned by the female of society. Men thus are funnelled into being in a relationship to avoid this stigma. Which is very good for society.

There is an element of truth to the expression: "You educate a woman and you educate a generation." Women are the safety fuse of society. They play such a vital role in regulating both men and other women. A huge reason Western societies are the way they are is because of the influence the female of those cultures has on them.

If you got rid of all the men and left the women, society would continue to function. But if you got rid of all the women and left just the men, there would be carnage. Women play a very important role in regulating men. Women are essentially the regulators of men within society. That they are quick to stigmatize plays a huge part in society's sustainability, especially western societies.

The most dangerous men are those men that don't care what women think of them.

In society's where women's influence diminishes, those societies are either more violent or more authoritarian.

Part of the reason the male suicide rate is much higher than the female suicide rate is because when men make mistakes they are not forgiven. As in women ostracize them. But as I suggest, this ostracization by the females is very good for society.

I suspect that the reason there exists so many male psychopaths and sociopaths, is to counter how quick the female of society is to ostracize. It takes the pathology of a psychopath or sociopath, to be able to live with ostracization.

Life is like an assembly line in a factory. Part of that process is education, which entails teaching the young child, not just Maths and English, but also that they must grow up and have children themselves. This point I feel was not explained clearly in my previous notes: Remarks On Existential Nihilism (which is my own fault). When I said that the violence in marriage is generally ignored by the system, compared with escorting, what I meant is that it is ignored for a damn good reason, and that is because marriage produces children, which is as I assert, a vital part of the assembly line that is the economic system.

What I was attempting to suggest is that the violence in love is conveniently ignored, not because love is "romantic," but because love produces children. Despite all its violence and abuse, the system is biased towards love. Then the individual reacts to this bias and lack of stigma.

There is a bias from the system towards love (with respect to escorting,) not because they want you to be happy, but because love produces children. This bias thus creates a positive feedback loop with regards to a relationship: The system is biased towards it, which makes people adopt it, which in turn adds to its bias, which in turn leads to more people adopting it and so on.

Love is only romantic because it is not stigmatized. Stigmatize love and its romance would evaporate.

Urbanization contaminates love. We form relationships with those who everyone else loves.

Stigma really plays a huge role in forging societies. Both in our professional life and private life. For example, with our professional life, we try to work in a good job, especially if you are male. As in the male that works in McDonalds on the till is generally rejected by the female of society. Second, with regards to our private life, as in being in a relationship, that too is moulded by stigma to an extent. The male who does not get married is thought of as odd and perhaps a sexual deviant; then the female is funnelled into being in a relationship because she is not stigmatized sexually when in one.

Hate towards certain groups is vital for society. For example, the hate people have for sex workers, prevents women becoming sex workers and men visiting them, both of which benefit society. The outrage fuels the stigma. The more outraged society is about a certain something, the more stigma there is towards those who commit that certain something, and hence the less chance other people will commit the act themselves.

There is a cultural bias towards love and then men and women alike react towards this. What I am trying to infer is that because love lacks stigma, this makes it attractive for people. It is a way to manage one's presentation to society.

Just like the religious fanatics, the relationship fanatics cannot accept anyone or anything that questions their life choices. Anything that questions romance must be violently opposed and ignored. Just like a religious creationist.

If you want to know what controls you, look at what you would be laughed at if you criticized it. What am I attempting to suggest controls people? The answer is love. If you were to criticize love, if you were to remark that love is what the system uses to sustain itself, that it is how the environment takes advantage of people, you would be ridiculed, to the point that people would recommend that you be sectioned.

The amount of people for whom life is a competition. They must outcompete their peers as to who is living the best existence. Thus, they have to be married. And this is a waste of time because at the end of the day, when you die, no one will care how rich, beautiful, successful or happy you were in life. It, as in life, will just soldier on as if you never existed in the first place. Your greatest foe as Nietzsche said is undoubtedly yourself. But by that same token, your greatest saviour is also yourself, if only you can allow yourself to be.

Women do, from a sociological vantage point, hold considerable power over society. That Western countries are generally the places people desire to live, is only due to the influence that women have in these areas. Women control men, just as men control women. Men desire to be liked by women and to do that they have to behave in such a way that is labelled positive by the female of the herd. If they commit a crime, they will be shunned by the females of society. Even if they are law abiding, but choose never to marry, they are in ways again shunned by the females of society. Another way to think of it is that if you removed all the women from Western society and just left the men, the deviance rate would rocket.

Why do women seem to have such high standards when it comes to choosing a partner? Part of the reason is because they stigmatize men so intensely, that it causes them to demand such high standards in return. I have said it already, in that a consequence of you gossiping about other people, is that you become conscious of trying to avoid being gossiped yourself. You condemn yourself through gossiping about others, because you don't want others to gossip about you, as you do them. So if you are a woman, gossiping about another woman's boyfriend or husband, then you learn that in order to not be gossiped about by other women, to attain a partner who is really in demand. Thus you artificially create high standards in what you seek in a potential partner.

Just as women are flocking in their droves to the plastic surgeon office, men are desperately trying not to be shunned by the females of society. The former is the response of women's desire to be approved by men. The latter is men's desire to be approved by women. The society you see around you is the product of both sexes' ability to potentially label negatively. And in every interaction with people, we try our best to avoid a negative label, often unconscious.

People will fight to defend love because in truth they are defending their right to have sex and be labelled positively at the same time.

Western society is inherently patriarchal. We could easily train women to be billionaires or geniuses, but that damages society. If women are billionaires or geniuses, they are less likely to have children. So instead we train men to be the billionaires or geniuses, and groom women to be the wives and mothers.

The economic system and its ostentatious affluence soils love. Love only exists through suffering and solitude.

A couple who have only known affluence and success, when they hit a hurdle, their relationship disintegrates and rapidly at that. In contrast, the couple that struggles in life, flourishes. Fifty years after they first met, they are still together. Suffering is the glue that binds love together.

Love does exist, but modern society has corrupted it. In a sense, to genuinely love, one must distance themselves from modern society, which admittedly is difficult to do.

Which comes first, the chicken or the egg: Is it not stigmatized because we choose it or do we choose it because it is not stigmatized? For example, marriage. Do we choose marriage and this leads to us not stigmatizing it? Or is it not stigmatized in the first place and then we choose it because of this? I think the answer lies in the functionality of the state. And the state in the case of marriage is biased towards it, which then compels people to adopt it as opposed to other systems.

Ironically, in western societies, it is the women in most relationships that hold the aces. If they did not, western societies would collapse. What women in western societies possess is freedom of choice. They can choose to get married and choose who to marry. Part of the reason they continue to get married is because they are getting the better deal than the men. They control the relationship in most cases. Only five percent of men are in high demand, as in those 5% have women throwing themselves at them. If that were 95% of men that were in high demand, the system would collapse, simply because then the male would hold the aces. He could dictate the terms of the relationship. "If you don't do this, then i will dump you for another woman." Most men do not have that luxury. They are lucky to even have one woman like them. Thus, it is the female that holds the power: "If you cheat on me, I will divorce you and you will struggle to find another woman." But if as i suggest, that 95% of men were in demand, then women would be less likely to take the chance of having children. It would be too risky to do so. Their partner could just leave at any time and go off with another woman. But in the real world only 5% of men have such a luxury. To re-assert, in western societies, where women have the freedom of choice to get married and have children, the fact that those societies continue to flourish is only because in most relationships it is the women that hold the superior hand.

The flawed marriage is one where the husband must keep succeeding to be loved by his wife or the wife must remain beautiful to be loved by her husband.

Modern capitalistic society has putrefied love, success, happiness and most of all, the individual themselves.

The femicide rate is largely ignored by mainstream society. It just goes to show the bias from the system towards marriage and love. This bias is not because they want you to be happily married. It is because they want you to have children.

The man fears being a financial object; the woman fears being a sexual object.

Men are driven more by sexual desire than presentation management and the reverse is true for women. Society should be grateful for this, for if the female chose sexual desire over presentation management, that could be troublesome.

Make the men not as smart, so they will be biologically driven by sexual consumption. Make the women smarter, so that they will be sociologically driven by image. Men are raging sociopaths and women are raging sociologists. Men want physical sex; women want the symbol of the family unit. That is how society thrives.

Women are vastly more driven by what society will say of them than men. Which is very good for society.

I should have explained this better in my previous notes Remarks On Existential Nihilism. The reason you have fewer female geniuses than male geniuses is because of society and not biology. One must begin to see the effects society has on the young female who is essentially groomed to become a wife and mother by forty. In fact, you have more above average intelligence females than above average intelligence males. So why then don't these females take the next jump to genius? A huge reason is because they are primed through various sociological forces to be a wife and mother and not a genius. For example, Emmy Noether is considered one of the greatest mathematicians of the twentieth century. And she never married or had children. Einstein famously called her the greatest female mathematician of all time. The moral is, if you want to be a genius or a billionaire or both, don't get married and have children.

Women then retort that it has been their dream from a young age to be a wife and mother. These women assert that there is no societal manipulation. But this is just like the billions of people who dream of being rich film or music stars. The reason they think like this, the reason these are their dreams and aspirations, is because of sociological grooming. Grooming, that I must assert we are utterly oblivious to.

The End: Labelling and Gratitude

"Beware of overconcern for money, or position, or glory. Someday you will meet a man who cares for none of these things. Then you will know how poor you are." - Rudyard Kipling

I saw a question asked once on a forum on the internet: Why are most people not grateful? The answer is because society in order to sustain itself makes people narcissistically material in nature. As in, it is difficult to be grateful within society, because society is always trying to prevent you from being grateful. Through labelling, society makes you defective. The good news is that once you achieve maturity, life immediately becomes better. The bad news is that this does not happen overnight. It takes at a minimum two years to mature and it can only be done in solitude. As Rollo May testified, one does not mature painlessly.

One must remember that the reality is that life ends in unbearable pain for us all. So it is most important to have been happy prior to the end. To spend your entire existence miserable or unhappy and then to have to suffer at the end, is the worst possible path your life can take. So you have to choose happiness and the way to do this is to be grateful. Gratitude is the greatest retort to society.

But Self-help books do not work. This book or any of my books will not make a dent in people's lives. And it is not because the self-help books are of a poor quality, but rather because the conditions in life do not change regardless of what inspiring book you read. By conditions I mean exposure.

If you keep exposing yourself to society, you will be defective.

So, what can one do? The answer is that one should try to be grateful despite society. You may live in a suburb and you may work in an office with fifty people, but try to hone an attitude of being grateful, despite what life throws at you. And gratitude is an attitude. It is a personality disorder in reverse. And the sooner you adopt this attitude, the better your life will become. As I suggest, the solution is to be grateful despite society.

Gratitude is simple, but the difficulty lies in mastering the simple.

The End